FIRST PRINCIPLES

OF

ETHICS.

DESIGNED AS A BASIS FOR INSTRUCTION
IN ETHICAL SCIENCE

IN

SCHOOLS AND COLLEGES.

BY

J. T. CHAMPLIN,
PRESIDENT OF WATERVILLE COLLEGE.

NEW EDITION, REVISED.

BOSTON:
WOOLWORTH, AINSWORTH & CO.
NEW YORK: A. S. BARNES & CO.

STEREOTYPED AT THE
BOSTON STEREOTYPE FOUNDRY.

PREFACE.

THE favor with which my text-book on Intellectual Philosophy has been received, and the need which I have felt in my own classes of a similar book on Ethics, have induced me to add this to the many excellent treatises on that subject already in existence. The great enlargement of the list of studies in our schools and colleges, of late years, renders it more desirable than ever that text-books should be brief, presenting only essential principles, to the neglect of details, which may be supplied by the teacher, or by general reading. These considerations have determined the form of the present treatise.

At the same time, I have hoped to present a more orderly outline of the principles of the science, and supply a more rational foundation for them, than has usually been done in treatises on Ethics. The doctrine that right is conformity in conduct to the nature and reason of things, is not, indeed, a new doctrine, but it has been a good deal overlooked of late, and has never, perhaps, been fully and consistently carried out. Whether it has been in the present instance or not others must judge.

Aiming at an orderly and consecutive development of the principles of the science, I have introduced the opinions of others but sparingly into the text. These have generally been reserved to the end, where they have been presented together, in the form of an Historical Abstract, which, it is hoped, will be found both interesting and profitable.

WATERVILLE COLLEGE, July 1, 1861.

CONTENTS.

FIRST PRINCIPLES OF ETHICS.

CHAPTER I.

ACTION AS THE SUBJECT OF ETHICAL SCIENCE.

1. *Ethics a practical science.* — Ethics, or moral philosophy, — the one designation being of Greek and the other of Latin origin, and, as now used, meaning precisely the same thing, — is a *practical* science. Not that ethics is any less theoretical than other sciences, — for every science is necessarily a theory, — but it is a theory pertaining to practice, and for the sake of practice. The term *practical*, therefore, refers wholly to the object-matter and end of the science. Ethics, then, even in theory, is entirely practical in its scope, since it sup-

plies us with principles by which we may deter mine the right in each case. Hence what is commonly called *practical ethics* deserves this name, by way of distinction, only because it actually applies these principles to the various relations of life, and deduces hence a general code of morals for the benefit of those who have not the intelligence or the leisure to deduce, in each case, their duty for themselves.

2. *It is the science of the laws of right action in the individual.* — Ethics, then, treats of action. It does not, however, treat of action in all its aspects, nor under all relations. It treats only of the acts of intelligent beings, and, indeed, as it is a human science, only of human acts. Its principles may, or may not, apply to the acts of other intelligent beings; it is enough for us to know that they apply to ours. And of human acts, in strictness, it treats only of those belonging to man as an individual, unchanged by any of the artificial arrangements of society, and personally responsible to the right from the very nature which

God has given him, and the circumstances and relations under which he has placed him. Ethics is thus the science of the conditions or laws of right action in man as a moral agent. The science of right conduct in man, as a member of civil society, and as far as his duties are modified by the special arrangements of such society, constitutes what in propriety is called *political philosophy*.

3. *It views acts only as right or wrong.*— Acts present themselves to us under various aspects, as awkward or graceful, agreeable or disagreeable, civil or uncivil, proper or improper, wise or unwise, and the like; but moral philosophy treats of them only as *right* or *wrong*. It is true that some of the other distinctions of acts here named, or which might be named, approach in significance the distinction of them into right and wrong, and may in certain cases be substituted for that, but not generally. They are none of them equivalent to it, nor necessarily even of a moral nature. Thus, a right act is, in one sense, always a proper act; i. e.,

it is proper or suitable to the situation and nature of the agent; but an act may be proper according to various other standards which have nothing moral in them. So a right act is always a wise act; but every wise act is not necessarily right, as it may be deficient in the end to which it is directed; it may be wise for its end, but that end a bad one. And so in other cases. The distinction of right and wrong, then, is peculiar, if it is not indeed wholly independent of all others.

4. *Right and wrong defined.* — The words *right* and *wrong* are terms in general use, as applicable not only to action, but equally to other things; as in the expressions, "All is right," "Every thing goes wrong," and the like. Now, we are warranted by the general principles of association, upon which the variations in the sense of words depend, in assuming that there is a common meaning running through these terms in all their different applications. What, then, is the fundamental idea expressed by each of them? *Wrong*, as

is well known, is only another form of the word *wrung*, and hence denotes what is "twisted," "deflected," "turned out of the way." In like manner, *right* (from the Latin *rectus*) means "straight," "without deviation." Here, then, we have the fundamental meanings of the words; and these meanings, in substance, they must retain, whatever the objects to which they are applied. Hence *wrong* always implies a departure from some assumed standard, and *right* conformity to it — which standard, in the case of actions, as we shall presently see, is the nature of things.*

5. *Moral right and wrong.* — Natural right and wrong, then, form the basis of moral right and wrong; or, more properly, right and wrong in their nature are fundamentally the same in all cases — moral right and wrong being distinguished from right and wrong in general

* This paragraph and a few others have been transferred from an article on Moral Philosophy furnished by the author for the April number of the Christian Review for 1860.

only by the object-matter to which they pertain. The term *moral* is derived from the Latin *mores*, meaning "conduct," "character," etc. Moral right and wrong, therefore, are simply natural right and wrong as exhibited in conduct. But as right and wrong in conduct are praiseworthy or blameworthy, — since we are always liable to temptations to depart from the right, — moral right or wrong, when attributed to an agent, implies innocence or guilt. Hence we say of one who acts according to the best light which he can obtain, that he is morally right, (i. e., innocent,) even when the act which he performs is in itself wrong. But the right and the wrong of acts in themselves are the same in nature as the right and the wrong in any thing else.

6. *Action defined.* — An action, as far as it is external, consists of certain outward signs or motions, varying in different cases according to the nature of the act. And as every event has its relations to other things, so every act has its bearings uoon other things. It stands

related to nature, to the actor, and to other beings. As an expression of the internal principles and state of the agent, — and only in so far as it is such an expression is it his real act, — it shows his character, while it has its bearings upon the interests and rights of others, as well as upon the truth of nature and history. All this is included in an act as an object of moral approbation or disapprobation. The act is considered not merely in itself, as an isolated event, but in its totality of elements and surroundings — in its bearings upon the actor and other beings and things.

7. *The motive, intention, or purpose of an act.* — But, it may be said, we form our judgment of the moral character of an action, not from the act as a whole, nor from this in conjunction with its bearings, but from the motive, intention, or purpose apparent in the act. Very true. But what is the motive, intention, or purpose of an act? Every act commences from within, and is wholly determined in its character by the internal element. The agent

desires a certain thing, which he contemplates in his mind, and resolves to effect by a certain external act. When this external act is the natural and usual expression of the internal state of the agent, we gain from it a correct notion of his real act. But the external act may be resorted to only to deceive — to indicate one thing while the actor really means another. When this becomes apparent to us, we no longer regard the outward act as his real act, since this is not what he had in his mind and wished to accomplish; i. e., it is not what he *intended*, *purposed*, or what really *moved* him to action. The motive, intention, and purpose, therefore, are all the same thing, regarded from different points of view, and indicate the real action — indeed, are the real action. The external act, when not the natural expression of the internal state of the agent, is merely a blind; the real act is understood only as we learn the motive. Of course, then, we judge of an act according to its motive or intention, for this is the act.

Hence the motive, intention, or purpose has no significance except as showing what the real act is. The motive is not a mere quality of an act; it *is* the act, or at least shows what it is.

8. *Illustrations.* — Suppose a man wishes to go to Congress, and sits down to consider what he shall do to gain his object. His purpose is single, viz., to go to Congress; but the means of compassing it are various. He may either betake himself directly to electioneering, in which case his acts interpret his purpose, or he may resort to some indirect means to make himself popular, and secure the votes of his fellow-citizens — as to deeds of charity to the poor, or to the advocacy of religion or learning, or some other great public interest which will be likely to secure him the favor of the people. Now, in all such cases, his purpose remaining the same, the act is really the same. He resorts to these indirect means only because he thinks them likely to be more successful; but they are none the less electioneering acts on

this account. Of course, then, when his purpose once becomes evident, we judge of his acts accordingly, and as all the more unworthy because accompanied with deception, and deception, too, at the expense of virtue itself. So, if one should kill a mad dog at large in the streets, he would seem to have done a good deed; but should we ascertain that what he really intended, or what in fact moved him to discharge the missile or gun by which the dog was killed, was that he might, under this pretext, kill some other animal belonging to a neighbor, which the dog was passing by, we should condemn the act as wrong.

9. *Intentions and intended acts.*— We thus see that the real act is internal, and that the external act, whether the natural expression of the internal purpose or not, is none the less the carrying out of that purpose, and hence is to be wholly interpreted by it. So, too, if there be only the purpose of some act, provided that purpose be settled and deliberate, and no external act; as where one lies in wait

to murder or rob another, and finds no opportunity of doing the deed, we hold him as guilty as though he had accomplished his purpose. The actual performance of the act does, indeed, bring it home to us with greater vividness, and make us realize it more fully; but, when we calmly consider the case, we are unable to distinguish between the guilt of an evil act deliberately purposed, but accidentally prevented, and the same act carried into effect. But if the evil purpose be but half entertained, or only a transient thought passing through the mind, we hold the individual guilty only as he voluntarily retains and cherishes it. The least dallying with evil thoughts is reprehensible, and always tends to become habitual.

10. *Character as right or wrong.* — Character, meaning literally *an engraved outline*, is, if I may so speak, the particular form of each individual mind, the state and attitude of its active principles at any given time. A principle of action is that which prompts us to act; and the particular relation and subor-

dination of such principles in each mind constitute the individual's character. Knowing any one's controlling principles, we know his character; and knowing his character, we know how he will act under given circumstances. Principles of action, then, considered as tendencies to certain kinds of conduct, are naturally judged of as right or wrong, while the sum of them in any individual (i. e., his character) leads us to approve or disapprove him as a moral agent. We consider every one a good or a bad man according to his character, not only as shown in his acts, but as embracing certain principles of action. Hence the complete object-matter of ethics is action, including the intention or motive, as showing the real nature of an act, and active principles or character, as leading to such and such acts.

CHAPTER II.

ACTION PRESUPPOSES ACTIVE PRINCIPLES.

1. *Human acts are conscious acts.*—Action, as we have seen, proceeds from within, and hence presupposes active principles. Our acts are our own, self-caused and independent, and not merely the result of action in other things. Human acts are conscious acts, springing from and guided by internal principles. A machine acts blindly, from the influence of some impulse external to itself; but man acts only as he thinks, and feels, and wills, and in consequence of his thoughts, and feelings, and volitions. For each of these classes of mental energies, as we shall see, is concerned in action.

2. *How our powers of knowing are con-*

cerned in action. — By experience we learn what is agreeable, wholesome, good, and are so constituted that we can but desire and strive after what we have found to be such. But, at the same time, we are capable of experience at all only through knowledge. We move among objects, and test or try their qualities only as we know them. We are pleased or displeased with objects only as our senses are employed in perceiving them, or our thoughts in dwelling upon them. Gratification is but the reflex of the natural and healthy action of our various conscious powers. The first impulse to action, therefore, presupposes knowledge. At the same time, the whole conception of an act, as well as of its bearings, and of the probable conditions of its success, is en tirely a matter of knowledge. It is only through knowledge, also, that we understand the acts of others. Hence knowledge, though not the moving impulse to action, is an indispensable condition to that impulse, and plays a prime part in every act.

3. *Feeling as concerned in action.*—As just observed, what we have learned through our different faculties of knowledge to be agreeable, we naturally desire and strive to obtain, while we as naturally avoid what we know to be disagreeable. And the reason of our desire or aversion is, that the one object is agreeable to us, and the other disagreeable. That is to say, we are moved to the various acts of life by something pleasurable or disagreeable, something desirable or undesirable, supposed to lie in different objects and pursuits. What we desire, or have an inward tendency towards, seems to us desirable; the mind feels some complacency or interest in it, and is moved towards it by this interest. Thus, feeling,—which, in its various forms, constitutes the agreeable and the disagreeable, pleasure and pain,—being the ground of desire, is always the first impulse to action. Mere knowledge leaves us cold and indifferent; it is only as the warmth and impulse of feeling are added that we are moved to action. Feeling alone

gives us such a sense of things as to draw us out after them.

4. *Connection of feeling and knowledge.*— Thus, while knowledge is the necessary basis and guide of action, feeling is the moving power to it. They are both indispensable to action, and, furthermore, are indissolubly connected with each other in our constitution. Feeling of some sort is the invariable concomitant of the exertion of all our conscious powers — pleasurable feeling of their normal and unimpeded exertion, and pain of their over-stimulated or restrained exertion. Not only is feeling connected with the exercise of our different senses, but with our various mental perceptions or thoughts. We have pleasurable and painful emotions, not only in seeing, hearing, tasting, and touching objects, but also in the recollection or thought of objects. We are affected almost as much by the recollection of comely or frightful objects, or acts of cruelty or charity, as we are by the perception of them. Our convictions of truth and duty,

also, are merely feelings connected with the perceptions of truth and duty. The *eureka* of Archimedes was but the spontaneous outburst of the thrill of joy which he felt at the solution of his problem; while the calm delights of an approving conscience, and the bitter agonies of remorse, are only the feelings connected with the consciousness of having done right or wrong. But our feelings may be discriminated into different classes.

5. *The selfish feelings.* — Self-love, according to the form of the expression, means the love of self. But self, as distinct from the conscious acts of self, is something of which we have no direct knowledge whatever. The self, then, referred to in the expression, can be nothing else than the conscious states of self. But of these conscious states, some are agreeable and some disagreeable. And, as we cannot love the disagreeable, the reference must be exclusively to our agreeable states of consciousness. Hence self-love is merely the love of the well-being or happiness of self. Certain states of

consciousness seem agreeable to us; we feel complacency and delight in them, and hence desire their continuance. At the same time, as we have already seen, we feel an interest in those objects or pursuits which we have found by experience tend to promote our happiness. We love our own happiness because it is agreeable, and other objects because they produce those states of consciousness which constitute the agreeable. The feelings thus arising, whether from the direct complacency which we have in our own happiness, or from that which we have in the objects or pursuits which we suppose calculated to promote our happiness, may be called *selfish feelings*, since they all spring from self-love. But what is commonly called *selfishness* is a faulty excess of self-love, leading one to a positive disregard of the rights and interests of others for the sake of self.

6. *The sympathetic feelings.* — We are not only interested in our own happiness, but the possession of a common nature with our fellows

gives us an interest in their welfare. Knowing from our own experience something how they must feel in different cases, we naturally enter into their feelings in some degree. Thus we "rejoice with those that do rejoice, and weep with those that weep." We also feel for others shame, danger, honor, resentment, and other sentiments, which we are conscious of ourselves under similar circumstances. And in general there is, accidental circumstances being out of the way, a kindly and sympathetic feeling among the different members of the race, which grows stronger the more nearly they are brought together by acquaintance, dependence, natural relation, etc. Prizing our own happiness above every thing else, we can but be affected in some measure by that of others. Nay, we cannot be wholly indifferent to the feelings of any creature which has but the lower elements of the nature which we have. "A merciful man is merciful to his beast." The sensitive nature, which the lower orders of animals have in common with ourselves, gives them a hold upon our sympathies. These sympathetic feelings, which draw men towards each other, and unite them in fraternities, nations, societies, are not selfish, since they have no reference to our own happiness, but to the happiness of others. They and the acts to which they lead may and do tend to our own happiness as much, if not more, than any other feelings and acts; but our own happiness is not their prompting cause or aim. The sympathy which leads one, at the risk of his life, to rescue a drowning man, does not surely spring from a regard to his own happiness, but from fellow-feeling with another. That men often pretend to act from such feelings, when they do not, is very true; but that men may, and frequently do, act from disinterested motives, is clear.

7. *Organic or vital feelings.* — There is also a large class of feelings, which, from being localized in different organs of the body, may be called *organic* or *vital feelings.* Such are the various sensations determined in our organs

by the influence or contact of external objects. Such, also, are the feelings arising from disease, disorganization, pressure, or the exertion of the muscles. Under this class of feelings, too, though of a somewhat different nature, belong the *appetites*, as hunger and thirst, since they consist in, or are accompanied by, certain organic feelings. In hunger, there is an uneasy feeling in the stomach, independently of the presence or thought of any appetizing object. Our hunger may suggest such objects, but they are not necessarily the cause of it.

8. *Sentiments.* — The feelings determined more strictly by mental perceptions are usually denominated *sentiments.* These are such as curiosity or wonder, awakened by what we perceive around us, and leading, in turn, to a closer scrutiny and study of these objects; the convictions of truth and duty, connected with the perceptions of the true and the right; the feeling of shame from the consciousness of having done a shameful thing, and of in-

dignation at the wicked acts of another; also, the sense of beauty and deformity arising from the perception or thought of comely or uncomely objects. In general, all the moral and æsthetic feelings, and all the more ennobling and rational feelings of our nature, belong to this class.

9. *Desire and will.* — As we have already seen, what we feel a delight or complacency in we necessarily desire — i. e., feel the want of, crave, or tend towards. Desire is thus a blind tendency towards something which seems to us desirable, and hence a tendency towards an act. But there may be many such desires soliciting us at the same time to different acts. Hence there may be before the mind the question simply of action or non-action, or of action in this, that, or the other way. In either case, a choice must be made. We may be determined in our choice either by the strongest impulse for the moment, by a simple regard to our own interest, or by a regard to what is right in view of all the con-

siderations in the case. But, however determined, when we have made our choice, the question is settled, and the final impulse to the execution is given by the will. Thus our feelings of interest in something produce a tendency towards an act, the tendency is allowed by the reason, and is carried into execution by the will.

CHAPTER III.

VIRTUOUS ACTION PRESUPPOSES THE FREEDOM OF THE WILL.

1. *We hold men responsible for their conduct.* — We all ascribe virtue and vice to each other. In like manner the Scriptures charge sin upon men, and address them as responsible to God for their conduct. "For we have before proved," says the apostle Paul, "both Jews and Gentiles, that they are *all under sin.*" We daily commend or condemn men for their acts, and assign them a place of respectability or of infamy in society according as we regard their conduct and character as right or wrong. And we do the same with ourselves also. We approve or disapprove our own conduct and character, according as we are conscious to ourselves that we are actuated by

right or wrong principles. So, also, we find our courts of justice hold men responsible for bad conduct, and regard any plea of temptation, at most, as but mitigating the offence, not at all as excusing it. Thus there is in society an all-pervading sense of human responsibility.

2. *Yet acts seem necessitated.*—That we act as we please, no one can doubt. The question is not, whether we can or not always do what it pleases us to do; we obviously never do any thing else than this. The question, rather, is, Can we choose what does not please us? Is not our choice and volition *necessarily* determined by what at the time seems to us the most desirable? In other words, Are we not always determined to action by what is to us the strongest motive for the time being? And by the strongest motive is meant, the preponderating influence in favor of the act over those against it, or in favor of a different act, arising from the inclinations, dispositions, convictions, and whatever else goes to make up the present state of the mind. Now, can the mind avoid choosing in accordance with this

preponderating influence? Perhaps one would say, Yes, I am not necessitated, in any case, to choose what seems to me the most desirable. I can choose directly the opposite of that in any case. But does not that opposite, in such a case, become the most desirable to you from your point of view? Does it not seem to you better to choose it than to choose any thing else? And do you not choose it on that account? You wanted to show that you could choose the opposite, and that at once became the preponderating motive with you for the choice. Whichever way we turn the matter, therefore, we seem to be necessarily determined in our conduct by the strongest motive; we cannot, in thought at least, escape the circle of necessity.

3. *It is, however, but a moral necessity.*— While we have no direct consciousness of any necessity in our acts, yet when we attempt to reason upon the nature of causation in a rational agent, we can but conceive such an agent as necessarily determined by the reason,

thought, or feeling which has the most influence with the mind. There is, however, this peculiarity in the case: no thought comes into the mind, or can exist there, alone, but is always associated with, and hence awakens, other related thoughts, thus presenting the different aspects of a case to the mind. There is a discursive power in the human mind, through which the part suggests the whole, the premise the conclusion, the cause the effect, the wrong the right; and in general, ideas related by similarity, contrast, or other ties, suggest each other. Each thought brings its related thought with it. Consequently, we need not be determined by any single view of a case, and hence not by the wrong view, unless our character is such as to give that view the greatest influence with us. But our characters being what they are, it may be said that practically the necessity remains. Let us see, then, what may be said to mitigate or obviate the objection drawn from this fact against human responsibility.

4. *Nor is it a very hard necessity.* —

Now, supposing the case to be just as it presents itself to our limited powers, and as we are compelled to think it, there are some considerations which go to show that the necessity is not a very hard one. In the first place, it is obvious that we always do just as we please. This no one denies, or can deny. Even though the choice be necessitated, yet it is none the less our choice. We have no consciousness of laboring under any necessity in the case, and are only convinced of it when we attempt to conceive and comprehend the nature of causation in a rational agent. Again, since we do as we please, it follows that our characters are such as we have willingly formed. They are the result of our previous acting, and this acting has been such, in each case, as we chose. We have made all the improvements which, under the circumstances, we thought best to make, and have fallen into only such faults or vices as we willingly accepted. What hardship, then, have we to complain of in this matter? "When

God visiteth us, [for our iniquities,] what shall we answer him?" Nay, we even condemn ourselves. However much we may be determined to action by passion, prejudice, wrong views, or wrong feelings, we really approve of only those acts which are dictated by the best light and the best feelings in our nature. Whatever temporizing, or conforming to momentary impulse or interest, false views or wrong feelings, there may be in our individual acts, on reflection we condemn all acts that are not justified by a true and rational view of all the circumstances of the case. Thus we find, as set forth so vividly by the apostle Paul, "a law in our members warring against the law of our mind, and bringing us into captivity to the law of sin which is in our members," and see our need of that spiritual regeneration which comes "through our Lord Jesus Christ," that our nature may be brought into harmony with our conscience.

5. *The necessitarian solution of the difficulty.* — It thus appears, that however recklessly

men act, they all feel that they *ought* to act on rational principles; i. e., that they *owe* it to the nature which God has given them thus to act. And as thoughts do not come into the mind or exist there alone, the right view of every case is always accessible to one, and is generally of itself suggested to the mind. Hence, to act from impulse, which is wholly blind, or from self-love, which is blind to every thing except self, against conscience, which surveys the whole case, is to act upon a *wrong* principle, and cannot be justified by any necessity of thus acting which one may have brought upon himself by indulgence. The wrong is antecedent to the act. Such is the necessitarian solution of the difficulty.

6. *The free-will solution.* — As we have seen, we have no direct consciousness of any necessity in our actions; it is disclosed to our view only by a subtle reasoning upon the nature of causation, and hence is wholly a logical result. May not the necessity, then, be only in appearance — a false conclusion reached by

attempting to employ our powers in reasoning upon a subject beyond their scope? This is certainly possible, and must appear probable, when we consider some other cases of a like nature. Thus, although no one can ever doubt the existence of *motion* in objects, yet we may, by a subtle reasoning on the nature of motion, seem to prove it to be impossible — since a body moving must, at every conceivable instant of time, occupy, or rest in, some portion of space, and hence its apparent motion is only a succession of rests; there has really been no instant when it was not at rest. There are many other fallacies of a like nature, especially in regard to our conceptions of space and time, which seem to arise from our attempts to reason on subjects beyond the scope of our powers; and it is probable that our reasonings against the freedom of the will are of the same nature. At all events, the fact of our condemning both ourselves and others for wrong conduct is evidence of our consciousness that we are at least practically free.

CHAPTER IV.

RIGHT ACTS MUST BE DICTATED BY INTELLIGENCE.

1. *Thought and feeling the real sources of action.* — Whatever may be the fact in regard to the freedom of the will, the will must somehow come to its determinations from what is before the mind. The only original sources of action, therefore, are thought and feeling — the will merely opening the way, and furnishing the final impulse by which acts are carried out. A tendency, to be sure, is not an act until it is approved or allowed by the will; but this allowance or choice is only a decision made up from data found in existing states of the mind. Acts, then, spring either from thoughts or feelings. In reality, thought and

feeling always go together; but intelligence and feeling exist in such different proportions in different cases, that some acts may be said to be the dictate of the one, and some of the other.

2. *Many act almost wholly from feeling.* — Most men exert their mental powers but feebly, barely enough to apprehend in the vaguest way common objects and common relations. But these perceptions, vague as they are, are sufficient to awaken various kinds of feelings, which, together with the spontaneous feelings of our nature, at once acquire the ascendency in the mind, and control the conduct. They hunger and thirst; they are warm and they are cold; they love and hate; they are gratified and displeased; they have desires and aversions; they feel for others' joys and woes; they have hopes and fears; they experience the peace of an approving conscience and the bitterness of remorse. Thought, in its nature, is silent and unobtrusive; and being exercised so feebly by them, they are scarcely aware that

they have any thoughts, and thus give themselves up almost wholly to the more engrossing and exciting perturbations of feeling. Feeling becomes a sort of sixth sense to them; indeed, it is well nigh a substitute with them for all the senses.

3. *Feeling, however, is but a blind guide.*— But feeling is no guide at all, except as it is a reflex of intelligence. In itself it is dark and blind. It bears no light with it, but at most only the reflection of a light. The feelings are right or wrong only as they are warranted or unwarranted by the facts of the case. Even our most amiable and humane feelings cannot be trusted as guides. Following the impulses of so amiable a feeling as gratitude, a judge might be led to an unjust decision in favor of a benefactor; or, following pity, a kind-hearted man might give to the distressed what he owed to his creditors. So indignation or hatred, while it may, under the stimulating influence of self-partiality, lead to revenge, may also prompt to the just pun-

ishment of evil deeds. These cases—and many more of the same nature might be adduced—show that feeling can be trusted as a guide only when it is warranted by a view of all the facts in the case. Gratitude is good when it does not lead to the violation of any other relations, and is evil when it does. The same is true of pity, hatred, shame, and all other feelings. There are cases where these are warranted by the facts in the case, and may be rightly followed, and cases where they are unwarranted and wrong.

4. *Yet it has an important office in action.*—As already stated, it is feeling alone which gives us that lively sense of things which impels us to action. The perceptions and conclusions of the intellect are clear, but cold; the warmth and impulse essential to action are added by feeling. And, when our intellectual views are correct, and adequate to the case before us, such is our constitution, that, in the natural course of things, feeling is furnished in kind and intensity just as it behooves us to *act.*

Thus a landscape spreads out before one, and he has the calm and serene emotion of beauty which fixes him entranced to the scene; or he finds himself unexpectedly upon the brink of a precipice, and he has the thrilling and agitating emotion of fear which causes him to shrink back and flee from the danger; or he commits, or sees another commit, an act of injustice, cruelty, or treachery, and he shudders with horror in thinking of it. There is, indeed, in our fallen state, a want of correspondence in the intensity of our feelings to the nature of the case, on moral and religious questions; but this is the result of a corrupt nature and corrupt practice.

5. *The so-called "moral sense" is mere feeling.* — Now, feeling, as the liveliest impulse to action, attracts our attention much more strongly than the operations of intelligence do, and seems, indeed, to perform the whole work. Thus feeling stands, in the popular mind at least, as the grand director of action and the true guide of life. Indeed, many philosophers

have fallen into the same error in regarding conscience as a "moral sense." This view wholly overlooks the *perception* of right and wrong, and gives the entire ground to the more obtrusive element of feeling. It relies upon the *sense* of duty given by feeling rather than upon its perception. But, as we have seen, there can be no feeling, or sense of things, except as they are first perceived. The view thus disregards the most essential element in the case — that which alone can justify and warrant the feeling. Hence its defenders have never been able to make the moral sense appear to be any thing more than a fickle, variable, and blind guide, as it really is. Feeling is a trustworthy guide to duty when it is authorized by the entire view of the case; not otherwise. To teach men, then, that it is a sufficient justification of their conduct to assert that they *feel* it to be right, without giving any *reasons* to show that the feeling is warranted by facts, is to teach a blind morality, and make men conscientiously obsti nate. Persons thus guided are often right, but they are often wrong also; and, not being required to look for any reasons for their feelings, they have no means of determining which.

6. *Conscience must embrace intelligence as well as feeling.*—The power, or powers, by which we determine our duty, is usually denominated *conscience.* This term has the same derivation as *consciousness*, from the Latin *conscientia*, and seems, like that term, to denote the intelligent principle in general, but only as employed about action, conduct, character. Bishop Butler usually speaks of conscience as a "principle of reflection," "a capacity of reflecting upon actions and characters," and in other terms of like import. And, as far as conscience is a perceptive principle, employed in apprehending and discriminating acts in their nature, there seems no good reason for regarding it as a faculty different in kind from our perceptive and reflective faculties in general. The apprehension and comprehension of acts in their nature and bearings, as we shall presently

see, require the exercise of the same cognitive powers which are employed in the apprehension and comprehension of other objects. So, too, the peculiar feelings of approbation and disapprobation connected with the operations of conscience are only a special class of sentiments consequent upon our moral perceptions. And they derive their peculiar character from the nature of these perceptions. The right is the most important and the most sacred of all things, and hence the feelings connected with its perception partake of the same character. As man is the great actor in this scene of things, and hence the great disturber of God's universe, if he acts wrongly, it is fitting that he should be endowed, not only with capacities for knowing the right, but with the most pungent and authoritative feelings urging him to its performance.

7. *Conscience as a perceptive power.* — Conscience is called the *moral faculty* because it has to do with the actions (*mores*) of men. And, taking action as the object of this faculty,

we may readily see that its perceptions are of the same general kind as those of our ordinary faculties of intelligence employed upon other objects. In solving the question of the right or wrong of an act, we employ our different faculties of intelligence just as in other cases. An action, as far as it is external, is observed by the senses, like any other phenomenon; and as far as it is internal, or a mere conception of the mind, is a matter of consciousness to us, if it be an act of our own, and if not, is judged of by the outward act, the situation of the actor, and the results of our experience generally, both with regard to our own and others' acts. In this way we form a notion of the different acts both of ourselves and others. At the same time, from our knowledge of the actor and his relations to other objects and beings, we perceive the bearings of his acts upon them, and hence judge of their suitableness or unsuitableness under the circumstances. When they seem suitable to the nature of the actor and his relations, we call them right, and when not, wrong. In conducting such an inquiry, it is obvious that we use only our ordinary faculties of intelligence. The peculiarity of moral questions arises wholly from the object-matter to which they pertain, and the special character of the feelings connected with our perceptions.

8. *Conscience as distinguishing man from the brute.*—If this be the correct view of conscience, man is distinguished from the brute, as a moral being, very much as he is as an intelligent being. To man alone, of all terrestrial animals, belong those nicer kinds of perception, judgment, and feelings necessary for the comprehension and appreciation of the subtle and complicated elements which enter into conduct and character. The intelligence of the brute is not of a high order enough to compass such questions, and hence he is not morally responsible for his acts. Thus Bishop Butler remarks, "It does not appear that brutes have the least reflex sense of ac-

tions, as distinguished from events, or that will and design, which constitute the very nature of actions as such, are at all an object to their perception. But to ours they are; and they are the object, and the only one, of the approving and disapproving faculty."

9. *Conscience and the law of the land.*—The laws and institutions of a state, like every thing else which is human, are liable to be wrong. This we should suppose would be so from the nature of the case; and we find the liability realized in fact in the history of every nation. In most nations, the institutions and laws are established, not for the good of the whole, but for the benefit of a few. Indeed, as yet there probably has not existed a nation on the face of the earth whose institutions were framed with the simple purpose of meting out even-handed justice to all. And if any institutions had been formed with such a purpose, they might fail of securing the end proposed, from short-sightedness in the framers. Now, as civil institutions and laws bear most

directly upon the interests and happiness of men, any injustice in them must be deeply felt by those whom they affect unfavorably, and, from sympathy with their fellows, by all just men also, even if they are not themselves unfavorably affected by them. Is it to be ex pected, then, that such laws will escape the indignant criticism of the sufferers or their sympathizers? Is there any thing so sacred in human laws that their merits may not be canvassed? The evils of open resistance to law are so great that one may not lightly resort to it; but he may, or rather he should, openly and persistently expose the injustice of all wrong laws; nay, where they directly enjoin upon him the doing of any thing *positively wrong*, openly refuse obedience, be the consequences what they may. Conscience is higher than law; and, in a clear case of conflict between them, the law must yield — at least, conscience cannot.

10. *Conscience and Scripture.* — Scripture does not profess to supersede conscience, but

rather comes to its aid by offering new light and additional sanctions to duty. It addresses man as knowing, in general, the right from the wrong, but as in danger of disregarding his duties, especially to his Maker, from the evil tendencies of his corrupt nature. While it presses upon men the general principles of humanity, — such as love to enemies and the like, which they are specially liable to neglect, — it most emphatically calls their attention to their duties to their Creator, whom they are so prone to forget and to regard as a God afar off, having no interest in their conduct, and requiring no service at their hands. And, besides thus coming to the aid of conscience in cases where we might know our duty from the light of nature, the Scriptures enjoin many positive duties at which we could not arrive by the light of nature, and, especially, disclose to us a plan of recovery from our sinful and lost state. Even Scripture, of course, cannot escape the scrutiny of intelligence. But since, in its specific character of revelation, it treats of the nature, plans, purposes, and requirements of an Infinite God, we may well distrust the ability of our finite powers to grapple with such subjects, and positively and authoritatively to pronounce upon their truth or propriety. We may, however, inquire into the historical evidence that the Bible is a revelation from God; for this is a subject wholly within the scope of our powers.

11. *Conscience, then, is supreme within its sphere.* — Conscience, as a perceptive faculty, as we have already seen, is only another name for the highest forms of our intelligence. It is our perceptive and rational faculties in their highest and most responsible exercise. As the capacity of knowing the right, as the clearest and strongest light within us, — seconded, as it is, by the most urgent and authoritative feelings, — it is the natural guide of our lives. It points to the path in which we should walk, and illuminates it as we advance. Of course, from the very nature of the case, we are bound to follow the strongest light

within us, and not to turn aside into darkness, which would be sheer folly and perverseness. That we have such faculties is evidence that it was intended we should exercise them. And, if we do exercise them, we must follow them, unless we prefer darkness to light. Every thought or feeling prompting to word or deed can be rightfully allowed only as it is pronounced right and good by our highest intelligence. Even piety, or the sentiment of reverence for the Supreme Being, becomes wild, fantastic, and cruel, — as liable to be directed to a false as to the true God, — unless it be under the control of intelligence.

CHAPTER V.

RIGHT ACTS MUST BE GROUNDED IN THE NATURE OF THINGS.

Different theories as to the ground of right and wrong.— Different theories have been held as to the ground of right and wrong; but they all resolve themselves into three, viz.: that this ground exists either, I. In the nature of man; or, II. In the nature or will of God; or, III. In the nature of things.* It is the design of this chapter to examine these differ-

* I omit here, as evidently only partial grounds of right, the views — quite celebrated, indeed, in the history of morals — that acts are right only as they tend to our own good, or to the good of others. These are really only the grounds of the particular virtues of *prudence* and *benevolence*, and will, therefore, be considered under those heads.

ent theories with the view of ascertaining, if possible, which is true.

I. The Ground of Right not in the Nature of Man.

1. *What is here meant by "ground."* — The ground of any thing is that in which it inheres, and where it is found or perceived. Thus matter is the ground of its properties. And hence, in a secondary or derived sense, the ground of any thing is that upon which it rests, and which supports it; as where we speak of the *ground* color in painting or embroidery, or the *grounds* of an argument, complaint, and the like. It is in this latter sense that the term is here used. The ground of right, then, is that upon which it is found to rest, when it is traced back as far as our powers can trace it; or it is the source whence we draw our reasons for it and defences of it. As the ground of a complaint is the reasons for it, so the ground of right is the reasons for that. Hence the ground here spoken of is either

that which supplies the reason for our perceiving the right, or that which furnishes the reason for its existence.

2. *Difference between the ground of knowing and the ground of being.* — The doctrine of "sufficient reason," as it has been called, teaches that nothing exists, or is known, without a competent reason — the one being called the reason or principle of a thing's existing, (*ratio essendi,*) the other the reason or principle of our knowing it, (*ratio cognoscendi.*) Hence, in regard to right, as in regard to every thing else, we may inquire either for the ground of its existence or for the ground of our perception of it. We cannot doubt that, if our faculties were competent, we should find a reason for each. We are sure that our faculties are competent to the inquiry in the latter of these two forms, whether they are to the other or not. Besides, this is the only view of the question which is of any practical importance to us, although the other is the one which has been the most argued by moralists. In treat-

ing of right and wrong as the ground of duty, we must treat of them as they are perceived by the human mind. By the "ground of right and wrong," then, is meant the ground or reason of our perceiving them.

3. *What is meant by saying that this ground "is not in the nature of man."* — As we perceive at all only as we have powers of perception,* in one sense every perception may be said to have its ground in our nature. Was not our nature a conscious or perceptive nature, nothing could ever be perceived by us. But, though all perception depends upon our having a conscious nature, yet some of our perceptions depend immediately and wholly upon that nature, so that we can give no other reason whatever for them, while others do not. Now, it is here asserted that our perception of right and wrong is not of the former kind, but of the latter. The former class of perceptions are called *intuitive*, the latter *dis-*

* "Perception," here, and generally in this treatise, is used in its largest sense, for *any mental apprehension*.

cursive. An intuitive perception is a direct beholding of an object, real or ideal, as something presented and standing immediately before the mind, and taken in at a single view. Discursive perceptions, on the contrary, are indirect perceptions, such as inferences, conclusions, and the like. Now, as these latter admit of some description, and may in some measure be accounted for by reference to the matter with which they deal, they may be said, by way of distinction from our intuitive perceptions, to have their ground in something out of our nature.

4. *Distinction of intuitive and discursive perceptions illustrated.* — Perceptions by the senses are intuitive, and may be said to have their ground wholly in our nature. When I look at one object, and it seems to me to be of the color which we call green, and at another, which seems to me red, etc., I can give no other reason for these perceptions than that my nature compels me to them — that I cannot perceive them otherwise. I might, indeed, say

that the objects themselves are green, red, etc., and I perceive them as they are, and hence my perceptions are determined by the objects. But this, though highly probable, I never can know, since our knowledge of objects is necessarily relative to our powers, and hence I cannot assert it positively as the ground of my perceptions. I do know that I am determined to perceive them so by my nature, and this is the only valid reason which I can give for the perceptions. As perceptions, then, they have their ground wholly in my nature. But, when I make an inference, or draw a conclusion, from a process of reasoning, I justify this conclusion by pointing out the steps in the proof, or by reference to material probabilities, according to the nature of the case. Hence this class of perceptions, as we do not refer for their justification to the constitution of our nature, may be said to have their ground in something out of ourselves.

5. *The perception of right and wrong not intuitive.* — And if the ground of right and

wrong is not in the nature of the human mind, according to the distinction just made, our perceptions of right and wrong must be discursive, not intuitive. And such, I am confident, they can be shown to be. If conscience be an intuitive faculty, or an intuitive exercise of reason, apprehending the right and wrong of acts, just as we apprehend the qualities of objects by the senses, then it would be just as absurd to ask one *why* he thinks such an act to be right or wrong as it would be to ask him why he thinks the sky to be blue. The only answer which he could make, in either case, would be, that he thinks so because it so appears to him. That is to say, he could give no reason whatever for his perception, but only allege it as a fact. There could be no reasoning, therefore, at all, on moral questions, any more than about colors. But, while we never hear one asked to give a reason for thinking this to be black, and that blue, we do hear men questioned continually about the correctness of their moral distinctions. Men are always disputing about the right and the wrong in conduct, or the principles of conduct. Besides, ethics is evidently a progressive science, whereas it should be stationary if our perception of the right is intuitive. The perceptions of the senses are just the same now that they were when the first human eye was opened on nature; and why should not the same moral distinctions be made by the most ignorant and the most enlightened, by the men of one age as by those of another, if they depend upon the direct perceptions of an internal sense, just as the qualities of objects do upon those of our external senses? Conscience, then, must be a discursive faculty. And the same appears from an account of the perceptions necessary in determining the character of an action, as given in the last chapter, (No. 7.)

6. *What it is which deceives men in this matter.*—What deceives men, apparently, in this matter, is, that the moral feelings, like all feeling, are of course immediate, or, if I

may so say, intuitive. When an act is seen to be right or wrong, or according to right or wrong relations, certain feelings in regard to it immediately spring up in the mind — we are attracted towards or repelled from it; we approve it or disapprove it. And, as the operations of our perceptive powers are silent and unobtrusive, and as we are not accustomed to analyze our states of mind, these feelings are all that we are conscious of — so much so, that, in speaking of things which are regarded as right or wrong, we commonly say merely that we *feel* them to be so. Thus, though the moral feelings exist only as the result of moral perceptions, yet, as the more obtrusive element of the two, they very naturally attract the chief attention, and stand in most minds as the sole indicators of right and wrong. It is thus, as it would seem, that the perception of right and wrong has come so generally to be considered intuitive.

II. The Ground of Right not in the Nature or Will of God.

1. *The ground of its existence may be the will of God, but not of its perception.* — Recurring to the distinction already made between the ground of the existence of a thing and of our knowledge of it, the nature or will of God may, perhaps, be said to be the ground of right in the former sense, since it is by the will of God that it exists. As all things exist by the will of God, right and wrong may be said to exist thus, but only as it is admitted, at the same time, that the elements of right and wrong exist in the nature of things; since right and wrong in us, whether in thought or deed, exist rather by the will of man. If the elements of right and wrong exist in the nature of things, as things exist by the will of God, so do these elements. In this sense, the will of God may be said to be the ground of the *existence* of right and wrong, while the nature of things is the ground of our *perceiving* them.

2. *Does the nature of God determine his own acts?* — If things exist as they do by the will of God, a still further question may be raised as to how his will or acts are themselves determined; or, in other words, how he came to make things as they are. Was he determined in creation solely by his own nature, or was he influenced to make things as they are by the consideration that such an arrangement of things is fit and proper? In either case, the universe would be but a transcript of his nature — being, in one case, the result of the spontaneous action of that nature, and in the other, of its action controlled by the proprieties of the case. The question, then, seems to be similar to, if it be not indeed precisely the same as, that which arises in regard to the freedom of our own will or action. If God acts independently of considerations out of himself, he is free in his acts; but if he acts from extraneous views, these seem to control and determine his acts. We cannot expect, therefore, to come to any clearer or more

satisfactory views on this point, in regard to God, than in regard to ourselves. In both cases, as far as we can make it out in thought, acts seem to be controlled rather than spontaneous, though we have a consciousness in regard to ourselves that we are free. The nature of God may, therefore, spontaneously determine his acts; but the reverse seems to us to be the case. In the former case, the nature of God might be said to determine the existence of the right; but in the latter, the right would determine the acts of God.

3. *The revealed will of God not the ground of right and wrong.* — As we have already seen, Scripture does not profess to impart to men their first notions of right and wrong, but addresses them as already possessing such notions, and blames them for not applying them in determining and practising what is right. It thus comes to the aid of conscience, rather than supersedes it. This must be obvious to any one who is familiar with the spirit and words of Scripture. It speaks of man as "a law

to himself," and as able of himself to "judge what is right." It exhorts men to practise "*whatsoever* things are pure," etc., (as though they were able of themselves to determine what is such,) "to add to their faith virtue, and temperance, and purity," etc., and "do to others what we would have them do to us" — all which supposes a capacity in us of judging what is virtue, temperance, and right conduct to others. Indeed, if the ultimate ground of right and wrong was to be found in the precepts of Scripture, we could have no conception of right and wrong in general, but only of certain things as commanded or forbidden. There are, indeed, some things commanded or taught in Scripture of the propriety of which we are incapable of judging, since we do not know all the reasons for them — such as baptism and the Lord's supper, the observance of the Sabbath, the necessity of sacrifice for sin, the efficacy of faith and prayer, and the like. These are revelations on the authority of God; and, as far as they are duties enjoined on us, are called "*positive* duties," since they are imposed by a lawful superior, who is supposed to see good reasons for them, although these reasons do not fully appear to us. All which is entirely analogous to the proceedings of a parent or teacher with the children under his care. He imparts lessons and lays down rules, which he expects them to receive on his authority, although they do not fully understand them in all their reasons and bearings. But great as is our indebtedness to Revelation for our knowledge of the higher and most important of all duties, as well as for the light and sanctions which it imparts to duty in general, it cannot properly be regarded as the ground of right and wrong.

III. The Ground of Right and Wrong exists in the Nature of Things.

1. *What is meant by the terms here employed.* — As we have already seen, the ground of any thing is that on which it rests, and, when applied analogically to spiritual things, means

the *reasons* on which any conclusion, feeling, or mental state rests, or that which accounts for it. It has also been stated that right and wrong, in this discussion, are considered only as perceptions of the human mind pertaining to human acts. How right and wrong, as elements in things, came to *exist*, is another question, upon which some suggestions have been made; but the only practical question for us is, how we come to the *knowledge* of them. Right and wrong, to us, are right and wrong as perceived by us in our own or others' acts. Right and wrong indicate a distinction in our perceptions of the character of different acts; and the question is, What is there in the nature of different acts which determines us to decide one to be right and the other wrong? or, in other words, What are the reasons for our decision drawn from the nature of each case? For an act is a *case*, a happening, or an event — or the purpose of an event — of a given character, both in itself and in its connections with, or bearings upon, other things. The nature of things, then, referred to, is the *nature of acts as bearing upon things*, or *of things as related to the act and the actor*—including, of course, not only things material, but sensitive and intelligent creatures, the actor himself, as well as all other beings affected by his act. Now, in this sense, it is asserted that the ground of the right or wrong of acts exists in the nature of things.

2. *The thesis proved.*—If our perceptions of right and wrong in acts are not intuitive, as it has already been shown that they are not, then they are discursive acts of the mind. In other words, our perceptions of right and wrong are judgments, or conclusions, formed from various considerations, aside from our peculiar mental constitution, which constitute their ground or reason. Whence, now, do we derive these considerations? It has been shown that they cannot be derived from the nature or will of God, which are the only conceivable sources of them out of ourselves, except the nature of things. The reasons for these

conclusions or judgments, therefore, must be drawn from the nature of things. There must be something in the nature of each act, considered in itself and in its bearings, which warrants the conclusion to which we arrive, or, at least, seems to us to warrant it.

3. *The thesis illustrated.* — In saying that the ground of the right or wrong of acts is in the nature of things, I mean very much the same as when it is said that the ground of truth is in the nature of things. Absolute truth depends upon the absolute nature of things, and truth to us upon nature as it appears to us. So the absolute right of acts depends upon their absolute nature and bearings upon things, and right to us upon their nature and bearings as they appear to us. As the elements which constitute truth are found in nature, so the elements which constitute the right or wrong of acts are found in the nature of things as affected by these acts. The elements of right are as plainly discoverable in the bearings of an act upon the nature

of things as the elements of truth are from the nature of things themselves. Our final appeal is to the nature of things in one case as really as in the other. This was expressed by the old English moralists in their formula that "right is accordance with the nature and reason of things." There is always a reason for a right act, which may be drawn from the nature of things as affected by it. A careful consideration of an act in its nature and bearings — if it be not an act indifferent in its bearings — will always disclose some reason why it ought or ought not to be done. This will be seen more clearly when we come to treat of the different virtues as embraced under Justice, Veracity, Benevolence, and Temperance or Prudence.

4. *Confirmation of the above view.* — This view is confirmed by the ready explanation which it affords of various moral phenomena, which appear as insuperable difficulties on the supposition that our apprehension of right and wrong is intuitive. For instance, there are

some acts which seem to us morally indifferent — as whether one shall stand or sit, walk or ride, and the like. And why? Because their bearings upon ourselves and others, as well as upon the facts of nature and history, are indifferent; the reasons for and against them, drawn from these sources, seem equal. Again, if acts seem to us right or wrong according to their bearings upon men and things, we see why it is that men's notions of right vary with their intelligence; since it is by intelligence alone that we arrive at the true conception of these, and of the kind of acts demanded by the nature or reasons of the case. From the nature of the relation between parent and child, reasons may be deduced for certain mutual duties. But a parent convinced that life is a curse would think the reason of the case required that he should leave the infant to perish; while he who regards life as a blessing would feel bound to rear it with special care. And the like difference would arise, from different views of the case, with regard to the treatment of parents, in their old age, by their children. And such we find to be the fact. False views of humanity and human relations lead to infanticide and parricide among savage nations, as truer views lead to the reverse of this among civilized and Christian nations. Thus it is that the moral code of a community is so much affected by its customs, education, and laws, since these tend to determine and fix our views of the nature and relations of men and things.

5. *Bishop Butler's view.*—But it may be said the above view is not in accordance with the teachings of Bishop Butler, confessedly the profoundest and most satisfactory writer on morals in the English language, if not in any language. There is, I admit, some apparent discrepancy between the above view and his, but it is scarcely more than apparent. His fundamental principle is, that vice is contrary to *human nature*, considered as an economy, or in the true relation of its parts; and virtue, of course, is following human nature, consid-

ered under the same view. But, in considering the nature of man as an economy, or system of related and duly subordinated parts, reason or conscience, of course, comes out the superior or ruling principle. The result, then, is, that the economy of man's nature makes conscience the guiding principle; and human nature, as a guide in morals, is nothing more nor less than conscience as a guide. Thus his theory, if not exactly the same as that advocated above, comes to substantially the same result. For, according to his theory, not only is the yielding to any of the lower principles of our nature against the dictates of conscience, wrong, or a violation of the proper order of our nature, but acts of falseness, injustice, cruelty, etc., are also contrary to our nature in being contrary to conscience, its representative faculty. In other words, reasons may be given against every species of wrong, and hence all wrong may be said to be contrary to human nature, as summed up in reason, or conscience. Now, this is precisely what is taught above — only it is there added that these reasons are always supplied by the nature of each case.

CHAPTER VI.

JUST ACTS ARE ALWAYS RIGHT.

What justice is.—Justice is one of the *cardinal virtues*, as they have been called, and is the most cardinal of them all. It is the foundation of all right character, and without it the other virtues are of little avail. Justice, according to its derivation,—from the Latin *jubeo* (*jussum*), "I command,"—is what may be authoritatively commanded. It presupposes a clear case, therefore, and strong and valid reasons on its side. What we bid or command men to do, we must feel that we can enforce upon them by the most cogent reasons. Now, as, according to the theory advanced above, every right act may be enforced by substantial reasons drawn from the nature of the case, justice, in its most general sense, may be said to comprehend all the virtues. And the term is sometimes used in this comprehensive sense; as when we speak not only of justice to others, but of justice to ourselves, of justice to truth, and even of justice to the distressed. But justice to ourselves is Prudence, justice to truth is Veracity, and justice to the needy, the distressed, etc., is Benevolence. It is better, then, to leave to each of these virtues its proper sphere, and under Justice to treat only of the rights of man as man, as based upon what is his *own*, and hence excluding all others. Justice, therefore, has respect to the rights of men, I. As to property; II. As to life; III. As to liberty; and, IV. As to reputation.

I. Justice in Regard to Property.

1. *Ground of the right of property.*— In accordance with the preceding view of right, I hold that the rightful owner of any thing can always show a reason for his claim, drawn

from the nature of the case, which no other person can — in other words, that, in the natural order of things, there is always a hand, and but one hand, to which every possession rightfully belongs; that when in this hand, it is in its natural place, and when not in this hand, it is out of its natural place. An article does not become property until it has been appropriated by some one; and when any one has thus appropriated an article, he is expected to prove his title to it; if disputed, he must be able to show a better reason why he should possess it than any one else can. If he has produced it by his labor from elements which rightfully belong to him, or bought it with his money, or received it as a free gift from some one, or taken it from the ocean or any of the great unappropriated fields of nature, no one can dispute his claim to it, i. e., contest his right to it on rational grounds. In his hand, therefore, it is in its right place. He holds it without a rival, and has the sole right of its disposal. No other person, therefore, can present any good reason why he should have the article without his consent; and, should one take it without his consent, he has just as truly removed it from its natural place as one would a tropical plant by transplanting it to the pole. It is evident, therefore, that the right of property is founded in the nature of things, and that rightful possession may always be defended on that ground.

2. *This illustrated.* — We appropriate only what we take to ourselves to the exclusion of others. Air, water, and sunlight, under ordinary conditions, cannot be thus appropriated, and hence cannot become articles of property. Of articles which may become property, some are easily appropriated, since, occupying but a small space, they may be directly clutched by the hand, or lodged in our houses or about our premises. Other articles, such as tracts of land, are not so easily appropriated. But, however appropriated, in order to hold the property securely, one must be able to prove his title. Now, if I find a nugget of gold on

an uninhabited island, or a piece of coined money in the highway for which no owner can be found, or take a fish or a pearl from the ocean, or a wild animal at large in the mountains, or receive an estate from a friend, or discover and enclose, or appropriate by other improvements, a portion of land owned by no one else, I have a reason, in each case, for my possession, or why the piece of property should be held by me, that no other man has. And it matters not whether it costs me much, or little, or no labor. I may find a piece of money in the highway while journeying, and another man may be journeying with me, and yet, if I see it and get possession of it first, it is mine, in case no owner appears, and not his. So that the original right of property depends upon *prior appropriation.* If I have appropriated an article which has never been in the possession of any other human being, or for which no owner can be found, I have a sufficient reason for retaining it against all others, and hence have a right to it. Most articles can be appropriated only by labor, and property is improved only by labor; hence, in general, labor is the proper representative of value, but it is not the ground of the original right of ownership, unless it can be shown to have been bestowed on the article *before* it came into the hands of any one else. Labor simply changes or transmutes previously existing materials or elements; it does not necessarily impart the original title to them. As the representative of value, it entitles the laborer to the value conferred, but not to the article itself if previously possessed by some one else.

3. *Importance of the right of property.*— Every right is important because it is right. We cannot show the importance of any thing more effectually in any other way than in showing it to be right. If the right be simply accordance with the nature of things, it must lead to the good. The right, conspiring and harmonizing with nature, must lead to good results. Conduct guided by the right is

no longer at cross-purposes either with nature or the God of nature, and must end well. But we can see directly many of the advantages arising from the sacred observance of the right of property. Where the right of property is not generally admitted and strictly observed, capital can never accumulate, as no one will attempt to accumulate what may at any moment be taken from him. It is only as each one is allowed to retain unmolested the fruits of his labor that industry is developed and property accumulated. And without capital and industry there can be no progress in a community. Men improve their food, clothing, dwellings, lands, comforts, conveniences, and all which enters into the notion of civilization, just in proportion as each one is left in the undisputed possession of what is his own.

4. *The right of each to what he needs.*— But, it is said, as God has given existence to every man, it must be that each human being has a right to at least as much as is necessary for his subsistence. But how has he a right

to this? God has not only given us our existence, but he has so constituted things that the means of continuing this existence can be obtained only by labor. If no one labors or puts forth any kind of exertion, there must be a total want of all means of subsistence. Now, labor being the condition of subsistence, it is a condition to one just as much as to another, and no one can rightfully say to another, You work, and I will eat. This is not the order of things which God has established, but rather that "he that will not work, neither shall he eat." Of course, if God has not given one the ability to labor, the condition does not hold in his case, and others should labor for him. The feeble, the sick, the disabled, the unfortunate, are the proper objects of the sympathy and charity of the healthy, the robust, and the successful. But of those who are able to labor, all are under equal obligation to do so; and, if one can say to any other, You work, and I will eat, then all may say so.

5. *What is implied in the right of property.*

— Property is what is one's own, and hence the right to it is exclusive. What is one's own cannot be another's. There cannot be two owners to the same thing or the same part of a thing. As far as one is an owner of an article, his ownership excludes all others. He has the sole right to its possession, therefore, and can dispose of it as seems to him best — under his responsibility, of course, to his Maker. No man may take and use it, or in any way interfere with his right to it, without his consent. He may himself bestow it upon another, either with or without consideration; and in so doing he conveys to the other, by the very act, the same exclusive right to it which he had. So he may part with a certain portion of his property for the advantages derived from civil government; but the government cannot rightfully demand of him any more than is absolutely necessary for the proper conduct of the government according to the compact under which he voluntarily lives. If it do, it is just as much robbery as though it were taken from him by a private individual.

II. Justice in Regard to Life.

1. *Ground of our right to life.*—If a man has a right to any thing, it is to his life. His life, surely, is his own, as against any other claimant. Like every thing else which we possess, it is indeed the gift of God; but, being a gift to the individual, it becomes his to hold under God—it is his, and not another's. It is his property, and the most valuable of all property, since without it no other property is possible, or would be of any avail if it were. Hence it is said that "all that a man hath will he give for his life." Life is thus not only a lawful possession of each one, but the ground and condition of all other possessions. No one, therefore, may lightly take the life of another—never, indeed, without being able to show that the other has forfeited his title to it, and that he is the rightful executioner.

2. *Justifiable homicide.* — But suppose that one is attacked by another from malice, or for the purpose of robbery or murder; may he not rightfully defend himself, and, if necessary, take the life of his assailant? The right of self-defence in general need not here be discussed. The only question to be considered here is, whether self-defence to the extent of taking the life of another is ever justifiable. To this question it may be answered at once, that, when it is obvious that the object of the assailant is robbery alone, the taking of his life would not be justifiable. The reason of the case does not seem to demand it. Life is more precious than money; and, if the robber will be satisfied with your purse, let him have it and go on his way, and rely upon other means of bringing him to justice. But where the life is aimed at by the assailant, the case becomes equalized, and it is life for life. In such a case, as one life is just as valuable to its possessor as another, the party assailed would seem to have sufficient reason for taking

the life of his assailant, since thus only could he save his own. Of course, it will not always be certain what the purpose of the assailant is, and then the duty of the assailed becomes doubtful; but when the purpose is clear, the duty is clear.

3. *Taking life in war.*—The whole history of the world shows that war is one of the greatest of the evils which have afflicted our race. It is the embodiment of the very spirit of ruin. It wastes the earth, crushes out every vestige of civilization which comes in its way, swallows up capital as in a vortex, stimulates the basest and fiercest of passions, and fills the land with desolation, sorrow, and death. So great an evil may not be incurred for every trifling cause. It can be justified only by the most urgent reasons. Wars of aggression, or simply for the purposes of national aggrandizement, can never be justified. Such wars are mere robbery, or rather murder for the sake of robbery. Wars to deliver ourselves or others from oppression may unquestionably be

justified in some instances, according to the nature of the case; as where the oppression is extreme, crushing out every thing which is valuable in life, or where it is an insuperable barrier to some great progress for which a people are prepared, and which they are able to make, if left to themselves. Defensive wars, too, are justifiable, when the assailed party are themselves right, and not the guilty cause of resistance or assault. In such a case, the question becomes, as in the case of a personal assault, one of life for life. But in most cases, national quarrels are as unnecessary and as unjustifiable as family quarrels or individual quarrels are.

4. *Taking life as a punishment.* — Life being the most valuable of all possessions, there can be no justification for taking the life of another, whether by the individual or by society, except when it is a case of life for life. The individual, as we have seen, may, in self-defence, take the life of another, when his own is in danger. So, it would seem, might

society rightfully take the life of one who has designedly and with premeditation taken the life of one of its unoffending members. The individual not having been able to defend himself, and having unjustly lost his life by the assault of another, it becomes the duty of the society to which he belongs, or rather of the government which represents that society, and which has been established to protect the citizens, to take up his cause and defend it. This is not to be done, however, in a vindictive spirit; and hence the retribution is not placed in the hands of the immediate friends, but in the hands of the government, who can look impartially at all cases. Still, the punishment inflicted, to satisfy the community, must correspond somewhat to the nature of the offence. The feeling of ill desert, which all have in such a case towards the offender, must be met; and this is adequately met, as I conceive, only by taking life for life. Punishments are undoubtedly for the good of society; but this is not the idea which prompts them, or which should determine them. This would be wholly disregarding the crime, by looking away from it to the interests of the community. The offender, in that case, would not be regarded as guilty, but simply as a scape-goat for the good of society.

III. Justice in Regard to Liberty.

1. *Ground of our right to liberty.*—Liberty is freedom to use our time, talents, and property as we choose. That this is the inalienable right of every human being is obvious. Every human being, not utterly demented or insane, has been endowed with the capacity of knowing, choosing, and acting for himself. One may have these capacities in a higher degree than another, but each individual has them in some degree. And, having been endowed with such capacities by his Maker, each one feels that he has a right to exercise them, and that he alone is responsible for their exercise. Next to life, liberty is held by all to be our most valuable possession. Hence the

language of the orator is barely the expression of the feeling of each one — "Give me liberty, or give me death." It may be true that many persons might be guided more wisely by others than they guide themselves, or are capable of guiding themselves. And should such persons become convinced of this, and *voluntarily* place themselves under the guidance of another, there could be no valid objection to such an arrangement. But, feeling their right to liberty, and ability to guide themselves, no one may deprive them of this right. Besides, it is to be recollected that men are extremely selfish; and if one was entitled to the guidance of others on account of his superior ability, that ability would inevitably be exerted in guiding them, not for their good, but for his own. Liberty, then, is the universal birthright of man.

2. *The wrong of slavery.*—If liberty is the right of men, slavery, of course, is wrong. Slavery is not only a theoretical denial to men of the right to the control of their time, prop-

erty, and talents, but is a practical enforcement of this denial. It is holding another human being as our own — one who has as distinct a personality and responsibility of his own as his self-styled master. It is nothing less, then, than a claim set up by one man to own the soul of another. There must, therefore, be continually rankling in the bosom of the enslaved a sense of injury, insult, and wrong. This makes him restless, vindictive, and unfaithful. Feeling that his master has no right to him, he feels justified in avenging the wrong to himself by any ill return which he can make. Conscious that he does not owe the service imposed upon him, he will, of course, perform it but grudgingly, and escape from it at the first safe opportunity of doing so which offers itself; nay, goaded to desperation, may even vindicate his right to liberty by destroying his oppressor. At the same time, the master, aware of this state of mind in his slave, and conscious of the wrong which he has done him, is rendered suspicious, overbearing, and cruel. It is thus that slavery, in its operation as well as in its conception, proclaims the unnaturalness and hatefulness of the relation.

3. *Defence of slavery from the Old Testament Scriptures.* — Slavery, like other forms of wrong, has existed in all ages. And it is obvious, from the Old Testament Scriptures, that it existed among the Jews. Nay, the writers of the Old Testament, while they do not by any means *justify* it, do not expressly condemn it. They refer to it as it existed, without attempting directly to interfere with it, satisfied with inculcating a general spirit of humanity, justice, and equality, in the sight of God, which would be sure in time to subvert the system. Besides, the type of slavery which existed among the Jews was one of the mildest. At most, it was but partial bondage. We learn from the earlier books of these ancient Scriptures, especially from the twenty-first chapter of Exodus, the twenty-fifth chapter of Leviticus, and the twenty-third chapter of Deuter-

onomy, that the servant was not without his rights, and not beyond the hope of freedom. He might be redeemed by his friends; he was not to be delivered up to his master, in case he escaped; if he was maimed or abused by his master, he was to be set free; if he was killed, his master was to be punished; religious instruction and worship were secured to him; and every fiftieth year all slaves were to be set free. Such a system of slavery, even if it were sanctioned by the sacred writers, could hardly be appealed to as justifying slavery as it exists in this and some other countries at the present day.

4. *Defence of slavery from the New Testament.* — But slavery as it existed among the Greeks and Romans, where Christ and his apostles labored and taught, was of a very different character, it is said. This is admitted. The power of the master over his slave, in those countries, was well-nigh absolute, involving even the power of life and death. And yet this system is recognized in the New Tes-

tament, and the relative duties of master and slave under it are prescribed. Granted. The duties enjoined upon the master, however, are only those of humanity towards his slave, not the duty of holding him in bondage; while the duty of obedience enjoined upon the slave is not enjoined as the duty of obedience to their parents is upon children,—*because it is right*,—but as an exercise of Christian submission, such as one may exhibit under the infliction of any other suffering or wrong. And this, for the same reason that the Christians of that day were required to submit to the powers that were, though that power was wielded by so great a monster as Nero. It was better to submit with Christian meekness, and thus exhibit their religion under its most attractive aspect, trusting to the silent operation of its benign spirit and precepts in general, than to resist, and incur the risk of the total subversion of their religion by the strong arm of masters and magistrates. But a religion which laid down the broad rule of duty, that "all things whatsoever we would that men should do to us, we should do even so to them," could not have sanctioned slavery in any way. Indeed, the general spirit of the New Testament, from beginning to end, is a constant rebuke to slavery. That the above account of the ground on which slaves are commanded to submit to their masters is correct, is abundantly evident from a passage in 1 Peter, ii. 18, 19: "Servants, be subject to your masters with all fear; not only to the good and gentle, but also to the froward. For this is thankworthy, if a man *for conscience towards God* endure grief, *suffering wrongfully.*" And there are many other passages to the same effect.

5. *Defence of slavery on the ground of inferiority.* — Slavery is the fruit of war, and hence combines this peculiar enormity with its own. The first slaves were probably captives in war. Indeed, from the nature of the case, men must be subdued before they can be reduced to slavery. No man submits to it un-

less he is obliged to. Slavery, then, in all cases, must arise from the triumph of the stronger over the weaker, and the abuse of that superiority in oppressing them. The enslaved, in this sense, are always inferiors — they are the weaker party, who have been pushed to the wall. But where is my warrant for enslaving another because I am the stronger? Does might make right? But in defence of negro slavery, in particular, it is said that they are an inferior race in intellect, and capacity of action, and self-control in general. Now, supposing this to be true, it cannot justify the enslaving of them, as long as it is admitted that they are men and have human souls. If they are men they are each under a separate accountability to God, and cannot, without gross wrong, be subjected to the will of another. That one has but small capacities may be a reason why we should help him along in the world, but not surely for enslaving him, and using what capacities he has solely for our own interest.

6. *Defence of slavery from the good which it has done to the enslaved.*—That slavery has incidentally done some good we need not deny, for God can make even the wrath of man to praise him. That Africans, by being brought to this country and confined to service in the families and on the plantations of civilized men, must necessarily be more or less benefited, is obvious. But would they not be much more benefited by a *voluntary* residence in such families? How is it with other foreigners who come to our shores, and go out to service in the free states? Is not their improvement far greater? Do we not see them, by hundreds and by thousands, speedily transformed from common laborers to land-owners, capitalists, head mechanics, professional men, magistrates, and even representatives in the councils of the nation? the like of which, from the nature of the case, can never happen to slaves. In a wealthy country, like ours, laborers are always needed; and let them come from all countries and all

climes, and in helping us they will the most effectually help themselves. But let us not go and stir up wars among native tribes for the purpose of capturing and enslaving such of the poor, helpless creatures as survive "the horrors of the middle passage," and are landed safely on our shores. Neither right, nor humanity, nor Christianity sanctions such a course. From whatever point of view we look at slavery, it is evil, and only evil, and that continually.

IV. Justice in Regard to Reputation.

1. *Ground of the right to our reputation.*— Reputation is as much a rightful possession as any thing else. It is in general the result of character, and as far as it is such, is the most costly of all our possessions. For character is the grand result produced in us by all previous thinking and acting; and hence, whether good or bad, is a most costly product. But a good name is a valuable as well as a costly possession. The descent to

infamy is easy, but the ascent to true honor and virtue is rare and hard. Well may it be said, then, that "a good name is better than precious ointment." This is what gives one currency in society, and places him in a position to exert his powers to the best advantage. It secures him the confidence of the community, and makes him the recipient both of their esteem and their favors. A man of character naturally receives the most important trusts. Important interests are committed to one only as his character is a guaranty that he will attend to them faithfully. Thus our success, as well as our happiness and general well-being in society, depends largely, and, as we might say, almost wholly, upon our good name. Hence our reputation is not only a rightful possession, but one of the greatest importance to us.

2. *Duty in regard to the reputation of others.* — A right on one part imposes a duty on the other. If each man has a right to his reputation, it is the duty of every other

man to respect that right. Reputation is a flower of the most delicate nature, and is, therefore, most easily blasted. Hence every man should deal tenderly with the reputation of every other man, and see that he do him no injustice on so vital a point. So great is the danger of doing injustice here, on account of the delicate nature of the subject, that it is generally safer, even where one's reputation is somewhat factitious and above his merits, to let time correct the wrong estimate, than to attempt to correct it ourselves. But where we know that there is an utter dereliction of principle in a man who passes in the community for a fair character, and is thereby securing their confidence and patronage, we are not at liberty to conceal our knowledge of his true character from the public. But even in such a case, we may not deal in vague suspicions, nor communicate even positive facts in malice, but only for the protection of the community.

3. *Ways of doing injustice to the reputa-*

tion of others. — Slander is the general term employed to designate an offence against the right of reputation. But this may be either a malicious and designed traducing of the character of another, or only a thoughtless and idle reporting of evil about a neighbor, — as in scandal or gossip, — or even the expression of a slight suspicion, or, less than this, barely an ominous silence. In all these ways the good name of another may be injured, and by the indirect methods of suspicion and silence, quite as effectually, perhaps, as by the more direct methods. A suspicion may easily be made to indicate more than the reality, and silence, where it might naturally be supposed one would be ready to speak, in case he could say any thing favorable, is the worst kind of slander. These indirect methods, therefore, are often resorted to by those who wish to slander, but do not wish to be open to the charge of having done so. They are, however, just as much slanderers as though they had spoken right out what they meant.

CHAPTER VII.

VERACITY IS ALWAYS RIGHT.

1. *The ground of the duty.* — Veracity being something which is required of each man, irrespective of the claims of others, and not, like justice, something which each may *claim* of all others, on account of his special ownership in certain things, it presents itself as a *duty*, rather than as a right. But it is our duty to do only what is right. Veracity, then, as a duty in us, must be right on some ground or other; and, as the rightness of it does not arise from the nature of the relations of men to any particular objects, it must arise directly from the nature of things themselves. Thus, in the most literal sense, the

virtue of veracity has its ground in the nature of things; for veracity is barely speaking and acting out things as they are. It is merely truth, reality, reflected in our words and acts — a strict conformity, in all that we do and say, to things as they exist. It may always be said, that such a statement is true, and such a one false, because it is according to, or contrary to, fact, reality, nature. When one states that to be true which he knows to be false, the first thing which stares him in the face is, that he has falsified fact. The man who is attempting to pass off a lie for the truth is confronted continually by the reality as it is, and feels condemned in the presence of injured nature.

2. *The utility of veracity but a secondary ground of the duty, at most.* — But some have regarded the evils of falsehood and the benefits of truthfulness as the ground of the duty of veracity. That veracity is in the highest degree useful, and falseness in the highest degree injurious, is very true. We believe

that all right is good, and all wrong evil: this, however, is not the ground, but the effect, of their being right and wrong. Suppose injustice were not harmful in its tendency; would it not still be wrong? Would not the taking by an indolent man of what an industrious man had earned be wrong, even though no evil consequences flowed from it? Every one must be conscious that such would be the case. So veracity is right irrespective of the benefits to society which result from it. It is true that we could hardly live in the world without veracity; but this is only because that departing from veracity is departing from nature, and hence must necessarily lead to evil. As to the right of the matter, the uttering of a falsehood would be just as wrong, if there were no being in the universe to be injured by it, as it now is. Still, as the capacity of happiness in others is a reason why we should promote their happiness, as far as we can consistently with sterner duties, the benefits springing from veracity may, perhaps, be said to be a secondary ground of the duty; but no otherwise than it is also a ground of justice. In strictness, the good of others is merely the ground of benevolence, which is subordinate to both justice and veracity.

3. *Falsehood defined.* — The false is the opposite of the true. Whoever, therefore, states what is not true, states a falsehood. But the false statement may have been made by the individual on the supposition that it was in accordance with fact. In such a case, we say that the falsehood is not *intentional*, and hence is not culpable. Indeed, such a statement is not false to the mind of the individual making it. He meant to state the truth, but was mistaken in regard to the facts in the case. We can blame him, therefore, only as it appears that he neglected the means at his command for ascertaining the truth. On the other hand, persons often convey a false impression in stating what is literally true. When the statement is made for the sake of

conveying this false impression, it is as much a lie as though the thing intended had been stated in so many words. But the use of common terms, with no intention to deceive, is not falsehood, even though others should misunderstand them. So our looks, gestures, motions, and even our silence, may be either true or false, according as they are intended to convey a true or false impression to others. Certain acts, motions, gestures, usually imply certain things, and are thus a sort of dumb language; they are a substitute for words, and are to be interpreted in the same way. It is as much a falsehood to give assent to a false statement by a nod of the head as it is to assent in words. And, on the principle that "silence gives consent," even the failure to speak, or an omission of part of the truth, may, in certain cases, convey a false impression as effectually as the most positive words which could be employed. In short, all intention to deceive is falsehood; and nothing else is falsehood, whether it deceives or not.

4. *Evils of falsehood.* — As each individual can know but a comparatively small portion of things for himself, we are dependent chiefly upon the statements of others for our knowledge. It is vastly important, therefore, that these statements should be reliable. Any considerable presumption against the general reliability of writers — such as would arise from even a partial infidelity to the truth — would leave us in uncertainty on the most important points. Besides, a general disposition to falsehood would invalidate all testimony before courts of justice, and hence no man's life, property, or reputation would be safe. And how could we get along in every-day life — in our questions and answers, our promises and expectations, our engagements and contracts — if there was not a prevailing regard for the truth among men? Such being the evils of falsehood, we see how important it is that every one should cultivate a habit of the most scrupulous truthfulness in all that he says and does. Small departures from the truth lead

to greater ones; "white lies" lead to those of a darker hue, till at length the mind becomes so beclouded that truth is scarcely distinguished from falsehood.

5. *Is falsehood ever justifiable?* — Some moralists have held that falsehood is allowable and justifiable under some circumstances, as, for instance, where we are attacked by a robber, and can escape only by a false statement. But, if falsehood is wrong in the nature of things, can it ever become right? If the object of the robber be simply to obtain possession of our money, it were certainly better to give this up to him than to pollute our souls with a falsehood. But we are under no obligation to say any thing to him whatever, whether false or true. If we think best to reply to him at all, the reply should be true; if we do not think best to reply, we risk the consequences, and should meet them manfully. If attacked by force, it may be right for us to defend ourselves by force — *but not by lies.* While, therefore, we are not always under ob-

ligation to tell all that we know on any point, nor even to say any thing at all, what we do say, or indicate in any way, should always be true.

6. *Promises, and the keeping of them.* — Promises are assurances given by one to another that he will do so and so. The keeping of a promise, then, is making good our word — i. e., making it true. It is, therefore, a question of veracity. When I make a promise, I promise a certain fact or result; and, in bringing about that event, I show my regard for the truth; while I show my disregard for the truth by neglecting to fulfil my promise. But one cannot accomplish impossibilities. Hence there is need of caution in making promises. Where we have every reason for believing the result to be within our reach, we may properly promise it; but in other cases, we should give only qualified promises. But should we, through carelessness, make a promise which we are not able to fulfil, we may be blamed, indeed, for our carelessness, but

not for falsehood. So, if we rashly promise any thing which, on reflection, we discover to be wrong, we may innocently disregard our promise. Right cannot, in any case, be attained through wrong. As to the sense in which a promise is to be kept, morally the man is innocent if he keeps it as he had good reason to believe it would be understood, and intended it should be understood, (not as he intended to keep it himself,) when he made it; though, when property is at stake, he may legally be held to fulfil his promise according to the common and fair construction of the language employed. What has been said of promises holds, of course, of *contracts*, which are but mutual promises, usually made with some formality, binding two parties.

7. *Promises confirmed by an oath.* — Such promises are required where a good deal is supposed to be at stake; as where one is called upon to testify before a court of justice, and thus holds in his hands, as it were, the life, property, or other important rights, of his

fellow-citizens; or is called to take upon himself an important office, in which the interests of others are largely committed to him. In oaths of *testimony*, the individual promises to "tell the truth, the whole truth, and nothing but the truth." This is required that the whole matter may be brought before the court, and no false impression be given by presenting but one side of it. If testimony is to be relied upon at all in courts, nothing less than the entire knowledge of the case possessed by every witness should be required. The confirmatory oath is contained in the words subjoined to the promise, *So help me God.* The whole declaration, to be sure, is called an oath; but it is simply a promise sanctioned by an appeal to God. And this appeal is of the most solemn nature, since it renounces all hope of *help from God*, both here and hereafter, except as the testimony to be given shall be exactly such as is promised. It were well if all who make this solemn appeal realized its full import.

8. *Propriety of oaths.*—Oaths are certainly sanctioned by the Scriptures, as even the Lord is frequently spoken of in the Old Testament as swearing by himself, (Isaiah xlv. 23; Jeremiah xlix. 13; Amos vi. 8,) and the judicial oath is expressly enjoined in Exodus xxii. 11. The apostle Paul, also, in Hebrews, (xvi. 13–17,) refers at length to the promise of God to Abraham, which he confirmed by an oath; and he himself often uses a form of protestation of the nature of an oath, as, "For God is my witness," "I call God for my witness," and the like. But, it may be objected, does not our Saviour say, "I say unto you, Swear not at all," etc., (Matt. v. 34–37)? The Quakers, and perhaps some other sects, regard all judicial oaths as forbidden in this passage, and hence refuse to take such oaths on any occasion. But a candid consideration of the passage must, it seems to me, lead to the conclusion that it does not refer to judicial oaths, but to the unauthorized and irreverent appeals to God in common conversation—what is

commonly denominated *profane swearing*. For although, in the oaths referred to in that passage, the appeal was in words made to "heaven," to "the earth," or to "Jerusalem," yet the Saviour considered them as equivalent to appeals to God. It seems that the Jews, supposing it to be less irreverent, were in the habit of swearing by these and the like objects, instead of God himself; just as Catholics, and indeed Protestants, often swear by the saints, as in the expression "By George," etc. There can be no doubt, then, that it is profane swearing, and not judicial oaths, which is forbidden in this passage. And, aside from Scripture, the importance of the interests at stake often requires that men should be pledged to truth and duty by the most solemn and binding form of asseveration which it is possible to devise. There can be no doubt, however, that the oath is often trifled with, by being administered in an irreverent manner, and in cases of so little importance as not to seem to require it. Still, the oath must always remain an important sanction to all who believe in the existence of God and in the retributions of eternity. Not that the oath places a man under any obligation to truth and duty which he is not always under, but it constrains him to them by a special, self-imposed liability of forfeiting the help and favor of God.

CHAPTER VIII.

BENEVOLENT ACTS ARE RIGHT IF JUST AND TRUE.

1. *Ground of the duty of benevolence.* — Benevolence is a duty because it is right, and it is right because the foundation for it is laid in nature. The capacity of happiness and misery in man — and, indeed, in all sensitive creatures — constitutes a reason, in the nature of things, for benevolence towards them. The pleasurable, the agreeable, we must, from the nature of the case, — simply because it is pleasurable, — prefer to the painful. Indeed, happiness is the great good of man, and misery his great evil. And does not this constitute a reason why men should promote the happiness of each other in all possible ways

within the bounds of justice and veracity? Does not nature point to such a course by making us capable of happiness and misery? And, corresponding to this capacity of happiness and misery, we find ourselves endowed with sympathetic feelings towards our fellows, which dispose us to make their case, whether it be one of joy or of grief, our own. Knowing the sweets of happiness and the bitterness of misery ourselves, we know what they must be to others, and hence can but "rejoice with those that do rejoice and weep with those that weep." We thus, from our very constitution, have something of the same feelings towards our fellows, in the varying fortunes of life, which we have ourselves in like circumstances. These feelings, to be sure, are very much blunted and modified by the hardening and perverting experience of life; but that there is a ground for them in our nature, and that, accidental circumstances out of the way, they do actually exist in some degree, there can be no doubt. Here, then, in the very nature of man, we find solid ground for the duty of benevolence.

2. *Relation of benevolence to the other virtues.* — Benevolence, in itself, is but a feeling. It is the kindly sympathy towards our fellows which springs from our making their case our own, in some measure, in the various experience of life. It supposes, indeed, a knowledge of their case, — of their joys and sorrows, — which, however, is only inferential, not a direct knowledge. We judge that others are affected thus and thus, under given circumstances, because we know that we are; and, judging thus, we have something of the same feelings which we ourselves have in like cases. Thus the feeling, as in all cases, implies knowledge of some kind. But this knowledge, though important, and a sufficient ground for the feeling, is not, even with the feeling, a sufficient ground for action. Right action, in all cases, must be approved by our highest intelligence; it must be pronounced right as a result of our best investigation of the nature of the

case. We must take into the account, not only the condition of the person sympathized with, but our own, and our relation to all other persons as well, before we can act rightly in the premises. Kindly *feeling* and a kindly bearing towards others are always demanded by the community of nature among men; but *acts of charity* must be warranted, not only by the condition of the recipient, but by justice to ourselves and to others. If one has nothing to give, or owes all that he has in his possession to some one else, or if by giving he would encourage indolence or vice, or in any other way injure the community, he has no right to give, however great may be the sufferings of the party. But we may often induce others to give who have the means, though we have none ourselves, and may always exercise kind feelings towards the distressed, and perform many kind acts even, without injury to ourselves or others. Hence benevolence, as an active principle, must always be restrained within the bounds of justice and veracity, if not, indeed, of prudence. It is certainly subordinate to the two first-named virtues.

3. *The production of happiness only a limited ground of right.* — We see from the above how unsound the principle is, which is so confidently put forward by many moralists, that the production of happiness is the universal ground of right. If this be so, then, in deciding any question of duty, we ought to pay no attention to any other consideration connected with the case, except the single one of whether the proposed act will be likely to produce more happiness than any other. But, instead of this being the fact, in questions of justice and veracity, we pay no attention at all to any supposed tendency in particular acts to produce happiness. This fact is forcibly expressed in the proverbs, "Let justice be done though the heavens fall," "Tell the truth and shame the devil." Justice and truth must be observed irrespective of all regard to their effects upon either ourselves or

others. The good of others is the special ground of the duty of benevolence; but this duty, as we have seen, is itself limited by justice and veracity. No one can have any doubt that the right will lead to the good, and hence that happiness will be the *result* of the right, though not, to us at least, its ground. The ground of right, as has already been shown, is in the nature of things; and things may have been made as they are because such an arrangement would lead to the greatest good; and hence the greatest good may have been the end of God in creation, and hence the ground of his action, and hence, again, in this sense, the ground of right. But the production of happiness, whether in the individual actor, or in a greater number, or in the whole, is not, and cannot be, the general ground of right for us, since we do not even refer to it in the greater number of cases, and should inevitably be misled by it if we did, as we are very poor judges of what would produce the greatest amount of happiness in so vast and complicated a system of things.

4. *Particular and general benevolence.*—Particular benevolence is kind feeling and kind action towards individuals; general benevolence, towards a larger number, or the whole. These two forms of benevolence, though prompted by the same general sympathetic feelings of our nature, are not always coincident. An act which would be kind to an individual is not always kind when considered in reference to a larger number. It is always kind to the individual to assist him whenever he is in distress; but, as such indiscriminate aid will tend to encourage indolence and vice, it is not always kind to the community. And where there is any conflict of this kind, from the nature of the case, the good of the many should prevail over the good of the individual. On this principle, as well as on the ground of desert, the punishment of individuals for crime may be justified. The community is unsafe without it, and hence no mercy

can be shown them. So, too, we distinguish between the happiness of the individual for the moment, or for a brief period, and his happiness for the whole course of his existence, and always feel justified in acting so as to promote the latter, even to the disregard of the former in particular instances. Hence we may rightly withhold relief from a person in great distress, when it is clear that relieving him will only tend to foster vices or habits which will inevitably involve him in still greater distress in the end.

5. *Importance of the virtue of benevolence.*— But benevolence, though by no means the whole of virtue, is yet a very important virtue. The sufferings and sorrows of men are great, and call loudly for sympathy and aid. Indolence and vice, natural defects or want of capacity, misfortunes, providential calamities, and the "inhumanities of man to man," involve thousands and millions of our race in unutterable woes. At the same time, the great majority of the race are living in a compara-

tively depressed state for the want of true enlightenment, true liberty, or true religion. There are, therefore, on all sides, demanding our sympathy and aid, the vicious, the imbecile, the unfortunate, the ignorant, the degraded, and the oppressed. Indeed, all men are proper objects for our benevolent regard, and may, under some circumstances, become proper objects for our active assistance. True benevolence prompts to the assistance of all in need of our help, as far as that can be done consistently with justice and truth. Within these bounds its scope is unlimited, and its objects, in every degree of need, are without number. It is, at the same time, the most universal and the most amiable of all the virtues.

6. *Conjugal, parental, filial affection, etc.* — The special affections of kindred and friends are usually treated as something quite distinct from the general principle of benevolence. But, if benevolence has its foundation in the kindly fellow-feeling existing among men, and

be but a general term to designate the work ing of those feelings under different forms, there seems no good reason for regarding the feelings of friendship, etc., as any thing more than special forms of the principle of benevolence. It is clear that our fellow-feeling for each other, or interest in each other, is increased by an agreeable acquaintance with each other. Men are attracted to each other generally by a common nature and a mutual sympathy. But some, from a greater correspondence between their natures, are specially attracted towards each other, and find particular delight in each other's society. They thus become familiar, and hence, as well as from the stronger affinities of their natures, are able to enter better into each other's feelings, and come to regard each other almost as another self. And, even where there is no special congeniality of nature, simple familiarity, from being much together, enables us the more readily to sympathize with each other, and thus creates a special interest between the parties. And, besides the interest created by personal attractiveness and familiarity, there is still another, called *gratitude*, arising from some special evidence of good will to us. Thus the peculiar relations of husband and wife, of parent and child, — the parent looking upon the child as but a part of himself, and the child upon the parent as his natural guardian, and hence sensible of his dependence and indebtedness for continual favors, — of friend and friend, of benefactor and recipient, develop the benevolent principle under various special forms, and bind men together by peculiar ties.

7. *What benevolence forbids.* — Justice forbids interfering with the rights of men, but benevolence forbids interfering with their happiness, except for cause. Both our own happiness and that of others, to be pursued rightfully, must be pursued within the bounds of justice and veracity; but, within these bounds, true benevolence not only teaches us positively to promote it, but forbids all interference with it. True benevolence revolts at

all injury or harm to others, as though it were done to ourselves. We may, indeed, sometimes refuse a fellow-being aid or gratification, out of regard to his greater good or the good of the whole; but we may not, in any case, interfere with his pursuit of happiness while he keeps within the bounds of justice and veracity — least of all may we interfere with it for our own gratification. We may not subject him to bodily sufferings and toils, except as he submits to them voluntarily for a suitable reward; we may not, on account of our greater physical strength, treat him rudely and harshly; we may not darken and pervert his mind by withholding knowledge or by wrong instruction; we may not corrupt his heart by indulging his evil passions, or making him serve in any way as an instrument or medium for the indulgence of our own. Having a soul ourselves, and being capable of attaining to a high state of virtue and happiness, benevolence requires that we should treat others as capable of the same, and aid them in attaining it.

8. *Cultivation of the benevolent feelings.* — Such being the nature and scope of benevolence, we see, at the same time, its importance, and the means of cultivating it. A virtue so extensive in its applications, so much needed in the world, and so amiable withal, should be assiduously cultivated and practised by all. Kindness is sometimes called *humanity*, because it is the legitimate fruit of true manhood, the evidence of a genuine sympathy with man as man. To cultivate benevolent feelings, therefore, we have need to forget ourselves, except as members of the common brotherhood of man. We should study the nature and wants of man in the light of our own, and learn to make his case ours. We should make ourselves acquainted with the condition of those around us, with their sorrows as well as their joys; we should dwell upon the spectacle of misery as it presents itself in large cities and among degraded populations, and think of the countless cruelties and tyrannies by which so many of our race are tortured and crushed to

the earth. By filling our souls thus with a true conception of the sufferings of our race, we can but feel some sympathy for them; and acting upon this sympathy will tend to increase it, till it becomes a settled principle of action. Being men ourselves, we should be interested in whatever pertains to man, and most of all in his sufferings. We should not turn away from men because they are filthy, diseased, disabled, degraded, and dying, but listen all the more attentively to their cry on this account. This is but the dictate of true humanity, as well as of religion.

CHAPTER IX.

PRUDENT ACTS ARE RIGHT IF JUST, TRUE, AND KIND.

1. *Ground of the duty of prudence or temperance.* — Prudent acts are wise acts considered solely with reference to ourselves, or some particular interest committed to us. Prudence, considered as one of the cardinal virtues, is a wise regard in all that we do and say for our own good. It weighs pleasures, and chooses the most enduring and satisfying. It is not carried away by blind impulse, but stops and thinks. As a principle of action, it does not look beyond self, but considers well the bearing of every act upon self, not only for the present moment, but for the future. A prudent act, therefore, is one ordered by

our highest intelligence, as far as regards one's self. Hence such acts, if they be neither false, nor unjust, nor unkind to others, must be right acts. The same conclusion follows from another view of the case. Prudent acts, as guided by intelligence, are a result of the triumph of reason over passion and impulse. They are thus, with reference to the lower principles of our nature, acts of moderation, self-restraint, or temperance. One can act prudently only by disregarding blind impulse, short-sighted views, and momentary gratifications. Now, to follow reason or conscience against these lower principles must be according to the true economy of man's nature; and this is shown by Bishop Butler in his "Sermons on Human Nature." Prudence, therefore, is our proper guide, within the bounds of justice, veracity, and benevolence.

2. *Relation of prudence to the other virtues.* — A prudent act, as implied above, in order to be right, must be just, and true, and kind. No act, not even the most amiable act of

benevolence, as we have already seen, can be right, unless it be just and true. As justice and truth are the habitation of God's throne, so they must be enthroned in every right act. Prudence without justice and truth is sheer dishonesty and low cunning. The subordination of prudence to benevolence is not quite so obvious. Prudence, to be sure, without benevolence, is mere selfishness; but so is justice, without benevolence, little more than hard-heartedness. Benevolence, then, seems to be a necessary supplement to every virtue, an ornament fitting every character. But where justice leaves no room for benevolence, as we have seen, benevolence must yield. Now, is it thus between prudence and benevolence? Is one at liberty to follow the dictates of prudence, in any case, at the expense of the happiness of another? Certainly not, any more than at the expense of the rights of another. Negatively, therefore, benevolence limits prudence; but, as the duty of positively promoting the happiness of others, benevolence is not paramount to prudence, if, indeed, it be co-ordinate with it. Although the happiness of others is really just as important as our own, yet our own, from the very fact of its being such, must always seem to us the most important, since we can but have a more lively sense of it than of another's. And this being the necessary result of the constitution which God has given us, it would seem to be right, between two acts, one of which would promote another's happiness just as much as the other would my own, that I should choose the latter. Thus, for instance, while one would always be under obligation to save the life of a fellow-being in danger of perishing, if he could do so without losing his own, he might rightfully save his own life, in preference to that of another, when it was not in his power to save both. Still, as in reality the happiness of one is just as important as that of another, we can find no fault with one who, in a case where both have the same interest at stake, prefers that of the other to his own;

indeed, we commend the act in him as noble, and indicating a rare superiority to selfish views. And, on the contrary, we severely condemn, and even despise, the man who will risk nothing for the good of another, however great his need or danger.

3. *Prudence is the fruit of self-love.* — Prudence is wisdom in action, and this, properly, only as it respects the actor himself. It is that wise and careful calculation of results, — that nice weighing and balancing of probabilities, circumstances, and chances, — which are necessary in determining how one may act, in each case, most to his own advantage. Prudence, however, does not look to immediate advantage alone, but to one's good on the whole; it is a wise regard for the future as well as for the present. It is not, therefore, a regard for the right in general, — it does not necessarily pay any attention to that, as far as others are concerned, — but only to what wisdom dictates in regard to ourselves, in each case. We cannot doubt that what is

really for our good on the whole will be for the good of others; but, short-sighted as we are, our wisdom is incompetent for determining such vast questions. Hence prudence can be our guide only within the bounds of the rights of others. Such being the nature of prudence, we see that it is wholly the fruit of self-love. Self-love, being a desire for our own good and for such objects or results as tend to promote it, prompts us to use the various powers with which we have been endowed in securing that good; and such a use of our powers, as we have seen, is prudence. Prudence, then, is a wise use of our various powers for our own good, and as a dictate of self-love. And, as the whole movement originates in self-love, prudent acts are selfish acts — good for ourselves, but not necessarily for others.

4. *The other virtues not inconsistent with self-love.* — Self-love, as a universal principle of action, is an unsafe guide in many respects, and especially is liable to degenerate into a

narrow selfishness, which leads one to suppose that any happiness which he may be the occasion of to others is so much deducted from his own. Indeed, it is extremely liable to descend even lower than this, and become so cautious and calculating for the future as altogether to overlook present enjoyments, and even produce the greatest uneasiness and anxiety with regard to what is to come — thus not only refusing present happiness, but substituting in its place a perpetual and ever-increasing uneasiness with regard to the future. What is more common than such a result? And what can show more conclusively the folly of such a principle of action as a general guide? How much better, in all cases, to follow the right, leaving the result with God! Then we shall always have the satisfaction of an approving conscience. Then, while prudence is allowed its proper scope, we shall, at the same time, be just, and true, and kind. Then our minds will be open to all the innocent enjoyments of life, by which alone self-love is gratified, and our own happiness secured. Is the satisfaction arising from "doing justly, loving mercy, and walking humbly before God," less than that arising from the pursuit of riches, honor, or power? Indeed, can there be any true and permanent happiness from any pursuits which are inconsistent with justice, truth, and mercy? An approving conscience is the universal condition of all solid peace and enjoyment; and this can be had only by doing right to others as well as to ourselves.

5. *Prudence requires self-control.*—Prudence, being wise action as far as we ourselves are concerned, requires coolness, deliberation, forethought. The prudent man must not act rashly, but stop and think. Now, the great obstacle in the way of deliberation is the excitability and violence of passion. As already stated, feeling of some sort is excited by almost every mental perception; and it is excited on the very moment of the perception. It does not wait for different perceptions to be

compared, and a wise conclusion to be reached, but is developed instantly, like the explosion of powder by the spark, and tends to precipitate the individual into immediate action. At the same time, it is blind as well as furious. It bears no light with it, but only force. We can have no prudence, therefore, unless our passions are under control. The man who rushes this way and that, and catches at this pleasure and that as feeling or passion prompts, is the mere sport of circumstances, and a thousand-fold more likely to act against his own interest than for it; indeed, if he acts for his own interest at all, it is only by accident. The fop, the glutton, the drunkard, the debauchee, the violent man, are as far from prudence in their conduct as they are from right. It is only when our passions are so under control that we can stop and think calmly, and act according to our best convictions, that our conduct becomes truly wise. Hence it is as important for ourselves as for others that our passions should be under due control.

6. *Prudence requires self-improvement.* — Prudence, being the fruit of self-love, must require of us progress in whatever is for our real good. Progress is the law of our being. The right exercise of the various powers which God has given us necessarily leads to progress. Progress, improvement, advantage of some kind, is the very end of prudence. Wise action is wise with reference to some end. Prudence in business is such a management of our affairs as is calculated to lead to the accumulation of wealth; prudence in conduct towards others is such an ordering of our conduct in public as is calculated to secure the respect, the honor, or the suffrages of our fellow-citizens. But the ground of all other improvements is the improvement of the mind and heart. Whether we consider it in itself or in its fruits, this is the chief good. A mind fully developed in its various powers, and a heart properly chastened and purified

in its sensibilities, are the greatest of all blessings. As the one enables us to understand the true and the good, so the other places us in full sympathy and communion with them. Self-culture, therefore, is demanded by prudence, as clearly as it is prompted by curiosity.

CHAPTER X.

ACTS OF PIETY ARE RIGHT IF DIRECTED TO THE TRUE GOD.

1. *What piety is.* — To the four cardinal virtues, Justice, Veracity, Benevolence, and Prudence, may be added Piety, which is a virtue, indeed, and something more than a virtue. In general terms, the sentiment of piety may be described as a disposition to reverence a Supreme Being. All men have some notion of a Supreme Being as the Maker and Preserver of the universe. This wondrous frame of things, these bodies so fearfully and wonderfully made, these souls with such astonishing powers, this mysterious principle of life running through nature, and this grand procession of things moving on with such

majesty around us, seem to imply the existence, behind the scene, of an almighty operating Agent. Our lives, our destiny, our all, are in the hands of this great and glorious Being. And not only so, but, looking into our hearts, we find sin there, and very naturally conclude, with the apostle, that, "if our heart condemn us, God is greater than our heart, and knoweth all things," and hence, for a stronger reason, will condemn us also. Thus the sense of sin is added to our sense of dependence, and conspires with it in producing that mingled sentiment of reverence, gratitude, and awe towards the Supreme Being, which constitutes the basis of piety. This sentiment, however, is crude and undefined in most persons, and leads to no rational worship or true obedience.

2. *How the sentiment of piety varies with our conception of the character of God.* — Piety is thus, in its beginnings, a mere sentiment, or feeling, springing from the perception of certain relations which we hold to God. And,

as feeling is dependent upon knowledge, the sentiment of piety must vary in its character according to our apprehension of these relations, or, what is the same thing, according to our notion of the character of God. For how do we form a notion of the character of God, if it be not from his supposed relations to us, and what we see around us? If we have any idea of God, it is as our God, as our Maker, our Preserver, our Benefactor, our Keeper, our Judge. Now, if we misapprehend these relations, and hence get a wrong notion of the character of God, our feelings towards him will be wrong. If we conceive him simply as the absolute Proprietor and Sovereign of men, exercising his power and authority arbitrarily, something after the manner of an earthly tyrant, enraged at his offending creatures, and demanding their humiliation, their punishment, their destruction, the sentiment of piety becomes little more than fear, filling the mind with gloomy forebodings, and prompting to wild, fantastic, and cruel acts of worship, such as prevail in most heathen nations. Whereas, on the contrary, if we regard God, as he is represented in Scripture, as our Maker, Preserver, and bountiful Benefactor, our gracious heavenly Father, "not willing that any should perish, but that all should come to repentance," the sentiment of piety assumes the form of love, gratitude, adoration. Thus piety, as a sentiment, can be right only as our conception of the character of God is right.

3. *How piety as a practical principle varies with our conception of the character of God.*— But piety is not merely a passive sentiment. As a feeling based upon our conception of the character of God, it must become to some extent a practical principle. As a practical principle, however, it still acts in its character as a feeling; it is simply a feeling or tendency allowed and carried out into act. Of course, then, it must still vary with our conception of the character of God. Hence it is that the religions of the earth differ so widely. For religion is but the embodiment of the senti-

ment of piety in acts of devotion, institutions of worship, etc. When, therefore, this sentiment is wrong, it embodies itself in wild and frantic acts of devotion, and in absurd rites and institutions of worship, such as we meet with in heathen lands; while in Christian countries, where the character of God is better known from Revelation, and especially from the revelation of himself made in Christ, religious duties, rites, and worship assume a more consistent and rational form. But even among Christian nations, and in the midst of the light of Revelation, the character of God, and hence of his requirements of us, are very extensively misapprehended. Fanaticism on the one hand, and religious indifference on the other, alike indicate defective views of God, and a defective sense of obligation to him.

4. *The ground of true piety.* — According to what has now been said, the ground of a true and rational piety must be sought for in the character of God. It must be a sentiment and practice inspired by a true conception of

his character. Now, whatever may be the real character of God, we can know nothing of it except as it is exhibited to us in nature and revelation. And from these sources we learn that God is the original Maker of all things, and of ourselves among other beings and things; that he sustains all things in existence by the constant exertion of his power, as he orders and directs them by a constant exercise of his wisdom; that his Providence embraces every movement in this vast scheme of things, and is ordered for the best good of his intelligent creatures; that he knows our thoughts, words, and deeds, and holds us responsible for the same; that, seeing us to be sinners, and under the condemnation of the law of right, he compassionates our condition, and has made ample provision for our recovery from our lost state; but that, although thus long-suffering and compassionate, yet, as our final Judge, he will by no means spare those who persist in sin, but consign them to their just doom in another world. Is there not sufficient ground in the character of such a being, and one standing in such relations to us, for the exercise of piety in its appropriate forms of love, obedience, and worship? There can be no doubt of this. But let us consider each of these exercises of religion separately.

5. *The duty of love to God.* — We are made to love what is lovely. Love is the strongest kind of complacency which we are capable of feeling in any being or object. What we love seems to us very dear and precious. A loved object has for us strong points of attraction, either on account of something in itself, or on account of some benefit which we have received from it. Hence has arisen the distinction between the love of complacency and the love of gratitude — the former denoting the love which we have towards a being on account of his character or personal excellences; the latter, the love excited towards a being on account of favors bestowed. On both of these grounds, we have the strongest reasons for the exercise of love to God. All that is lovely in

nature, whether in created objects or created beings, is but a feeble reflection of the loveliness of the Creator. And shall we love the copy, and not the original — the creature, and not the Creator? And what being in the universe has laid us under such obligations to gratitude as God? The favors of all others are but borrowed gifts, and limited in extent, while his are as original as they are unbounded. The very gift of being, which alone renders us capable of receiving any other gift, we owe to God, as well as all the subordinate gifts of life which go to make this being tolerable or happy. But God has made the strongest appeal to our gratitude in the provision which he has made for our recovery from sin through Jesus Christ. Well may an apostle say, "But God commendeth his love towards us, in that, while we were yet sinners, Christ died for us." Shall we not, therefore, "love him because he first loved us"? Accordingly, Moses, in giving that comprehensive command enjoining upon men love to God, — a command reiterated and enjoined anew in the New Testament,—says, "Thou shalt love the Lord thy God with all thy heart," etc., and calls upon each one, as a reason for the duty, to "*consider how great things He hath done for thee.*"

6. *The duty of obedience to God.*—"If ye love me," says the Saviour, "keep my commandments." And what is more reasonable—nay, what is more natural—than this? Love leads naturally to obedience. We always consider ourselves at the service of one whom we love in every thing which is reasonable. And infinite as our obligations are to God, we can hardly conceive of any service which it is possible for him to demand of us that would be unreasonable. The attitude of every human being towards God should be like that of the great apostle to the Gentiles, when, arrested by God in his mad career, and brought to his right mind, "he, trembling and astonished, said, Lord, *what wilt thou have me to do?*" Or, as the Psalmist has it, "When thou saidst,

Seek ye my face, my heart said unto thee, Thy face, Lord, will I seek." If we owe service to any being, we certainly owe it to God. If we are bound to respect the wishes and commands of any one, are we not bound to respect those of our heavenly Father? Now, the commands of God to us, as uttered both by the voice of nature and of revelation, are many and urgent. But obedience to these commands, so far as they are not a mere re-enjoining of the general duties of morality, and so far as it is necessary to consider them here, may be comprehended under the general duty of *worship*, which I now proceed to consider.

7. *The duty of worship.*—Worship, according to the derivation of the word, means an expression of our sense of the *worth* of God. It is, therefore, adoration, praise, intercession. A true sense of the greatness and glory of God, as "King of kings and Lord of lords," holding universal sway over all realms and

all worlds, fills the soul with the most exalted and irrepressible feelings, which spontaneously burst forth in such strains of adoration and praise as are found in some of the Psalms of David. At the same time, a sense of our own need, of our dependence, our ignorance, and, most of all, our sinfulness, impels us, as by an inward necessity, to fly for aid and pardon to this same glorious Being, who has revealed himself to us as a God of mercy and grace, as well as a God of wisdom and power. The various acts of worship, therefore, — such as adoration, praise, and prayer, — are the natural result of right views of ourselves and of God, and furnish a solid foundation for the general structure of public and private worship as observed in Christian nations. But true worship, be it observed, springs only from true views of God and of ourselves; and hence, while we need faith to enable us to apprehend God in his true character, and as ever near us, we need also a consciousness of our weakness and sinfulness to impel us to seek his aid and forgiveness. Such, as I conceive, is the nucleus of the religious character, from which, as a fruitful germ, spring alike the whole round of religious duties and the whole energy of the religious life.

CHAPTER XI.

ENVIOUS AND MALICIOUS ACTS ARE ALWAYS WRONG.

1. *Envy is a faulty excess of emulation.*— Emulation seems a natural consequence of our desire of self-development and progress. As each one has this desire, there is of necessity a universal struggle for the good which each one places before himself as an end, and hence an animated rivalry to see which will attain his end first and most perfectly. Now, as it is not only natural, but also proper, that we should pursue with our might any coveted object, provided that object be a worthy one, and should even be stimulated in its pursuit by the progress of others towards the same end, it is obvious that there is not necessarily

any thing wrong in mere emulation. Emulation, however, like benevolence and every other feeling, may be faulty in degree, and always becomes so when it is not warranted by the reason of the case. And especially does emulation become faulty when, not content with simply vying with others for the mastery in any thing, one attempts positively to hinder the progress of another by retarding or injuring him in any way. Here emulation passes into *envy*, which is always and necessarily wrong, whether as a feeling or a principle of action. It never can be right positively to injure another in any degree, or even to wish him evil.

2. *Malice or revenge is a faulty excess of indignation or anger.* — Anger, indignation, resentment, are words of similar import. They do not, indeed, mean precisely the same thing; but neither of them implies any thing which is necessarily wrong. Even anger, which implies more that is unreasonable than either of the other terms, is not always wrong, as is

plainly implied in that injunction of the apostle Paul, "Be ye angry, and sin not." There is an anger, then, which is not sinful. We may resent an injury, or be angry at the injurious person, or indignant at the wrong which he has done us, without committing sin. These are not only natural feelings, but may be justified by the nature of the case. It is right that we should resent an injury, though it may not always be right that we should undertake of ourselves to avenge it. However, such feelings are of the greatest service — nay, absolutely essential — in bringing wrong-doers to justice, and thus protecting society from destruction. They are, indeed, the special forms through which conscience expresses its condemnation of wrong and wrong-doers. But anger as a mere blind passion, a sort of fury of feeling without sufficient cause, is wrong, and so is resentment or indignation, when no injury is intended, or when the resentment or indignation is greater than the injury demands. And all of these feelings alike, when they pass over, as they often do, into ill-will and ill-doing to others, are always wrong. This will be evident from a brief exposition.

3. *The wrong of malice and revenge.* — Malice is wishing or intending ill to one; and revenge is inflicting evil for evil, or for supposed evil. Now, since, as already stated, our sentiments of anger, resentment, etc., act an important part in bringing offenders to justice, why may they not be allowed to act directly in effecting this result? Why not allow the individual to take the administration of justice into his own hands, and follow these instinctive feelings in administering it? This may be allowed where immediate action is essential, as in warding off sudden danger or violence, or where the state of society is such as to provide no better remedy. But in a well-organized society, provided with laws and courts of justice, the right of self-defence must be limited to those instances where, from the nature of the case, no other remedy is possi-

ble. We have a clear right to defend ourselves when our lives are endangered by the assault of another, and may be excused, perhaps, for the instinctive return of indignity for indignity prompted by the spontaneous action of resentment; but experience clearly shows that, in general, revenge, or the rendering of evil for evil, by the party injured, only tends to call forth revenge again in return, and so on without end, and in a constantly increasing ratio. Such a course, therefore, cannot be right. Experience has proved that legal remedies, in such cases, are far better; nay, even where there are no such remedies, it is generally better, except in extreme cases, to suffer wrong than to resort to such dangerous means of redress. And as to malice, or any form of ill will towards a fellow-being,—even against those who have done us the greatest injury,—it never can be justified. We may resent their wrong to us, and desire to have them punished for it, but may not wish them any real evil.

4. *The duty of loving enemies.* — Our Saviour, addressing his disciples, and, through them, us, says, "Love your enemies, bless them that curse you, do good to them that hate you, and pray for them which despitefully use you and persecute you." This has been regarded as a hard saying, and as enjoining a virtue too high for the attainment of so frail a creature as man. It is evident, however, that we can but regard it as a virtue, and a virtue of the highest and most transcendent character. But it cannot be a virtue for us if there is any impossibility in the case. Is there, then, any impossibility here? Must I necessarily be an enemy to one who is an enemy to me, or who has injured me? Certainly not. His happiness is not the less important because he has injured me, nor will my hostility to him help at all the injury done me. But, it will be said, we are so made that we can but resent a wrong done us. Very true; but resentment, as we have seen, is not hatred or ill will. A parent

may be indignant at a wrong committed by a child, or a friend resent an offence in a friend, and even assist in bringing him to punishment for the same, and yet have the most cordial good will to him all the time. We may, then, forgive injuries in others, and these being forgiven, the common sympathy existing among beings of the same race insures a residuum of good will towards the offenders, or real interest in their welfare.

5. *The duty of loving our neighbor as ourselves.* — The Scripture precept, that each should love his neighbor as himself, is a direct consequence of the principle, that the happiness of every other man is just as important as our own. This every one recognizes as a correct principle, and will admit, in general, that it warrants the duty. Theoretically, the duty seems plain. But how is it possible for such beings as we are to carry it out? Is it possible for us to love another as we love ourselves? Can we enter into the case of another so as to have the same

feelings, of any kind, for him, which we do for ourselves? It may be doubted whether, as far as intensity is concerned, the same feelings can be exercised by us towards another which we experience in ourselves in a like case. But we may have the same feelings in kind towards others which we have towards ourselves. And these feelings may be sufficiently strong to move us to act towards others as we should towards ourselves in like circumstances. And this, as I conceive, is what is required by the precept. We are required to have the same *kind* of regard to the happiness of others which we have to our own, and to act in a like way in the two cases.

6. *The duty of doing to others as we would that they should do to us.*—What has been called the Golden Rule of Scripture requires that we "should do to others as we would have them do to us." Here, what we demand of others is made the standard of our duty to them. Now, even if we take the rule in

its most unqualified sense, there is a sort of justice in it. We cannot, according to the rule, be unreasonable in our demands upon others, without laying ourselves liable to the like unreasonable demands being made in turn upon ourselves. The rule, then, is calculated to bring down our demands upon others to the standard of simple right and justice. Hence the true intent and meaning of the rule most unquestionably is, that we should do to others whatever we can *reasonably* demand that they should do to us. The standard of our duty to others, then, is not what our caprice or selfishness may require of them, but what the reason of the case would authorize us to require of them.

7. *The malevolent affections.* — The *malevolent affections*, as they have been styled, are the opposite of the benevolent affections, and are such as envy, anger, resentment, hatred, malice, and the like, already referred to. Some of these, as we have seen, are but faulty outgrowths of the others, and all of

them, according to Bishop Butler, are but secondary principles of our nature, having reference to the evils incident to an imperfect state of existence, such as is appointed us here, but not necessary to the completeness of our nature in a perfect state. If there was no such thing as wrong in the world, there would, of course, be no use for such a passion as resentment. But whether this be the correct account of these passions or not, it is certain that such of them as are not mere faulty excesses of the others, have nothing necessarily evil in them. As we have seen, they do not necessarily involve ill will to others, but merely impel to the resistance of wrong, and to bringing the wrong-doer to justice, and thus serve as a balance to pity, which would be likely to let the offender go free. Thus we see, that the wrong of our nature is not in its original principles, but in the faulty excesses to which we carry them. All the original principles of our nature are good, but many of them may be carried to excess, and all of them may be perverted from their proper use and purpose to serve the selfish ends of the individual. Indeed, selfishness may be regarded as the root of the corruption of our nature.

CHAPTER XII.

OBLIGATION TO DO RIGHT.

1. *Nature of moral obligation.*—We are now prepared to consider the nature of moral obligation. Obligation, as was remarked of the terms *right* and *wrong*, is a word of general application, and must have radically the same meaning in all cases. It denotes, according to its derivation, that which *binds* or *constrains* to something. It is not, however, a physical, but a rational constraint, which is referred to—the force of some consideration over the mind. A note of hand is called an *obligation*, because it contains a promise to pay, and acknowledges an actual indebtedness. So we feel ourselves obliged to

one who has bestowed a favor upon us, and thus created a balance against us. In like manner, moral obligation is only the constraint to a given act, or course of action, which arises from the reason or reasons that urge to it. It is obvious from the account which has been given of the ground of right and wrong, that it can be nothing else than this. The same is implied in the other terms employed to express moral obligation, such as *ought*, *duty*, etc. Ought means to *owe*, and duty implies a *debt*—what is *due*. Both words alike imply a balance against one; i. e., a deficiency, an incompetence to meet the case rationally, without performing the act in question. Moral obligation, then, is a rational constraint to a particular course of conduct, urged home by the most persistent and authoritative feelings of our nature.

2. *Moral obligation according to Butler.*—Bearing in mind what was said in an earlier chapter of the view of conscience taken by Bishop Butler,—that with him conscience is a

rational faculty, and is our natural guide in conduct, because it is the clearest and strongest light in our nature,—keeping this in mind, the above account of moral obligation is entirely consistent with that given by this eminent moralist in the following passage, found in his third Sermon on Human Nature: "But allowing that mankind hath the rule of right within himself, yet it may be asked, 'What obligations are we under to follow it?' I answer, It has been proved that man by his nature is a law to himself, without the particular distinct consideration of the positive sanctions of that law; the rewards and punishments which we feel, and those which, from the light of reason, we have ground to believe, are annexed to it. The question, then, carries its own answer along with it. Your obligation to obey this law, is its being the law of your nature. That your conscience approves of and attests to such a course of action, is itself alone an obligation. Conscience does not only offer itself to show us the way we should walk in, but it likewise carries its own authority with it that it is our natural guide — the guide assigned us by the Author of our nature; it therefore belongs to our condition of being; it is our duty to walk in that path, and follow this guide, without looking about to see whether we may not possibly forsake them with impunity."

3. *Obligation to the right arising from divine commands.* — Although the light which God has put within us must have been intended as our guide within its proper sphere, yet, being limited in its power of illumination, and in the extent to which its rays reach, it is not a competent guide in all spheres of duty. Our whole obligation to what are called *positive duties* arises from their having been enjoined by God. God is our rightful Superior, and may see reasons for many things which we are utterly incapable of seeing, and may therefore rightfully enjoin upon us duties the ground of which we are incapable of comprehending. So, too, the obligation to many

of our peculiar duties to God depends upon his special revelation of his character and ways to us, and is not, therefore, wholly derived from our unassisted reason. And, indeed, even the ordinary duties of morality derive additional sanction from being reënjoined in the Word of God. The child, from the dictates of his own conscience, may have a clear notion of his duties to his brothers and sisters; but when these duties are reënjoined upon him by his father, and upon the ground that they are all children of the same parents, he feels himself constrained to them by an additional obligation. So is it with the commands of our heavenly Father. They bring us all up, as it were, into his presence, and impress upon us anew, and with additional force, our relative duties to each other as members of the same great family.

4. *Obligation to the right because the right leads to the good.*—We must believe that virtue is consistent with our true happiness. We cannot conceive that the right should lead to

an evil issue, under the government of a perfect Being. A perfect government must, as a final result at least, secure the happiness of the righteous. And, as far as our experience goes, we see a tendency to such a result even in the present life. Although there is a sort of satisfaction in many kinds of sinful self-indulgence, still it is short-lived, soon loses its power, and even undermines the power of satisfaction from other sources. On the contrary, the satisfaction arising from doing right, and the exercise of the virtuous affections, though less exhilarating for the moment, is pure and unalloyed, and not only perennial itself, but opens and prepares the mind for the reception of ever-increasing satisfaction from all innocent sources. So, too, though the wicked, from the operation of artificial causes, often prosper for a time, yet, other things being equal, the upright, the honest, the virtuous, generally come out the best in the long run. Hence, even in the present life, virtue seems the surest road to happiness, and we feel certain that it must be hereafter. And, such being the case, it is obvious that it imposes upon us, as rational beings, an additional obligation to a virtuous life. As rational beings, we can but prefer what appears to be for our good to what appears to be for our harm. Hence, when the right is seen also to be good, we are constrained to it by an additional motive.

5. *Obligation to the right is no burdensome restraint.* — The obligation to do right is a rational constraint, and hence carries the whole mind along with it. To feel the obligation, in any case, one must be conscious of a preponderance of reasons towards a certain act or course of conduct, such as to silence all objections to its performance. Thus the "yoke" of duty, when really seen to be such, becomes "easy, and its burden light." But, in being constrained to the right, we are restrained, of course, from the wrong. A restraint is put upon our conduct by the law of duty. We are conditioned in all that we do by the right.

We must look out for the wrong, and avoid the wrong in all our conduct. The virtuous man must walk circumspectly in all things. But there is nothing in all this which makes the condition of the virtuous man so very peculiar, or places him at any special disadvantage as compared with others. No end can be attained without submitting to the condition — often very onerous — of using the appropriate means and incurring certain consequences. The practice of vice, therefore, as well as the pursuit of virtue, is conditioned. And, as Bishop Butler remarks, "With respect to restraint and confinement, whoever will consider the restraints from fear and shame, the dissimulation, mean arts of concealment, servile compliances, one or other of which belong to almost every course of vice, will soon be convinced that the man of virtue is by no means upon a disadvantage in this respect. How many instances are there in which men feel, and own, and cry aloud under the chains of vice with which they are enthralled, and which yet they will not shake off! How many instances in which persons manifestly go through more pains and self-denial to gratify a vicious passion than would have been necessary to the conquest of it!"

6. *Obligation to obey a depraved conscience.* —But suppose one's conscience be perverted, or rather, suppose one has a wrong view of a case, or a view which is not in accordance with the real nature of things; is he still under obligation to follow his conscience? Certainly. If moral obligation be a rational constraint to some course of conduct, a man must be bound to follow the best light he has, whether that light be the best possible or not. He is culpable, to be sure, if he has neglected any means at his command for obtaining correct views; but to go counter to his present convictions, however erroneous, would only be adding a sin of commission to a sin of omission. The man is just as much self-condemned who disobeys a perverted conscience as he is who disobeys an enlightened conscience. As

the apostle Paul says, "Whatsoever is not of faith is sin." Whoever acts against his best convictions, even though these be wrong, is himself wrong. He has violated the plainest dictates of his conscience, and can but condemn himself. In such a case, he is wrong in his acts as well as in his convictions; whereas, if he follows his conscience, even though perverted, he is right in his acts, and only wrong in his convictions.

CHAPTER XIII.

THE RIGHT, THE TRUE, AND THE GOOD.

1. *What truth is.*—We have seen what the right is; and it is now necessary, in order to point out their relations to each other, to learn also what the true and the good are. It is an old question, What is truth? Even if we accept that derivation of the term *truth* which makes it mean simply what one *troweth*, or thinketh, yet thinking (i. e., *thinging*, or dealing with things) is not mere imagining. All thinking consists in, or springs from, perceiving. Even the figments of the imagination are made up of elements received through the senses, and hence are regarded as having a likeness to the truth, though not the truth

itself. Real thinking, then, implies a real object of thought. Hence truth, even according to this derivation of the term, is thinking inspired by real objects. Truth, then, may be defined to be *the knowledge of things as they are*. It may, indeed, be objected to this definition, that, if nothing but the knowledge of things as they are constitutes truth, then we never can be certain that we have attained to the truth, since we never can be certain that our best knowledge of things is really an apprehension of them just as they are. As, however, we are constrained to believe that our knowledge, as far as it goes, is in accordance with the reality of things, and can never know that it is not, the perceptions of our senses, and the legitimate inductions and deductions from these, must be truth to us.

2. *Relation of the right to the true.* — Truth, then, as it seems, is a knowledge of things as they are, including not merely our perceptions of things external, but inferences drawn from these perceptions, when viewed under different

relations by the mind. The right, also, as we have seen, relates to things as tney are. Things as they are, within a certain sphere varying with the nature of the act, are affected by every action. There must be an appeal, therefore, to these things in determining the propriety or impropriety of every act. But they are appealed to only as known by us. In short, in determining the right or wrong of acts, we merely make use of our knowledge of things as far as it bears upon each case. The question, in every instance, is, Is this act warranted by the best knowledge which I have of the nature of the case, or of its bearings upon all concerned? The right, therefore, though differing from the true, is yet determined by it. Knowledge is not an end in itself. We are made capable of knowing the truth only that we may act according to it. Thus, while the right is determined by the true, it is, nevertheless, the end of the true. And hence the true end of life is not knowledge, but duty.

3. *What the good is.*—The good is of various grades, from the slightest momentary gratification to the chief good, the *summum bonum* of the ancient philosophers. Good is the opposite of evil, and is of two general kinds—natural and moral. Natural good implies happiness of some kind, or the means of happiness. Thus the gratification of any appetite or passion is a good; peace of conscience is a good; the acquisition of property, as the means of happiness, is a good; so also is the acquisition of knowledge a good. The good, in all these cases, is evidently happiness, or the means of happiness. When reduced down to what is actually intended, the good, in all such cases, turns out to be happiness, or satisfaction of some kind. Both property and knowledge are mere utilities, i. e., something to be *used* by us, and hence to serve us, in the pursuit of happiness. Nay, even the development of our powers and the perfection of our natures are but the means of happiness, or, at least, the occasion of it.

What is called moral good is right conduct and character. And it is so called, as I conceive, because right conduct is sure to lead to happiness in the end. Wrong leads to disorder and confusion, and hence to wretchedness; while the right tends to order and happiness. The former, therefore, is evil, and the latter good. And, since all temporary enjoyments and every species of happiness lead to misery in the end, unless they are in accordance with the right, moral good must be considered as the chief good — the real *summum bonum.*

4. *Relation of the good, the right, and the true.* — The true, as we have seen, is the real. The right and the good alike, therefore, have their foundation in the true. Without the true, neither the right nor the good could exist. The right, however, is directly and immediately determined by the true, while the good is only indirectly and remotely determined by it. While the right springs from the true, the good springs from the right. The true is thus the substantiating cause of

the right and the good, as the good is the final cause of the right and the true. Although the good, as well as the right, is possible only through the true, yet the true only exists immediately for the right, and ultimately for the good. Hence the true is the end of knowledge, the right of duty, and the good of faith and hope.

CHAPTER XIV.

THE NATURE OF VIRTUE.

1. *Of virtue in a restricted sense.*—Virtue, according to its derivation, means *manliness.* With the ancient Romans, *virtus* (derived from *vir*) denoted, almost uniformly, that manly courage which we call *bravery.* Being an intensely martial people, the courage to do battle with the enemies of the state, and face the foe, seemed to them the greatest human excellence—the highest proof of manhood. But there are foes within as well as foes without, and the resistance of these is a higher manliness than the resistance of external foes. As we have it in Proverbs, "He that is slow to anger is better than the mighty; and he that

ruleth his spirit, than he that taketh a city." Resistance to temptation, struggling against sinful inclinations or allurements to evil, is the best possible evidence of manliness, the highest excellence of which we are capable. Hence, in its specific sense, virtue differs from moral goodness — is, indeed, but a species of it. Thus, while we ascribe moral goodness to God, we never ascribe virtue to him. So, while we consider any right act performed by men as a good act, we hardly consider it a virtuous act, unless it is accompanied by some temptation to act differently. We often say of one who has told the truth, or performed an act of justice, Why, that is no evidence of virtue, since there was no temptation to the contrary. Thus virtue supposes a struggle with temptation, and a triumph over it. Indeed, although right conduct is always right and good in itself, yet it is only when the right is performed *as right,* — and to choose it distinctly as such implies some thought or temptation to the contrary, — that it has any special merit. The greater the temptation to evil, therefore, the greater the merit in acting rightly in any case. True virtue, then, is a triumph of good over evil. And such is the frailty of our nature, and such the temptations which beset our path, that right conduct in man usually partakes of the nature of virtue even in this restricted sense.

2. *Of virtue in a more general sense.*—But virtue is often used loosely to denote right conduct and right principles and dispositions in general. We often have occasion to speak of all moral excellence as one, and *virtue* is the term employed for that purpose. In this sense, it includes all right action, whether attended by temptations or not. Any right act may, in general, be said to be a virtuous act. But, even here, virtue refers more emphatically to right principles and right dispositions than to right acts. A virtuous man is one, to be sure, that acts rightly; but, more than this, he is a man of right principles, of right intentions, of right dispositions. He is not

only right outwardly, but inwardly. Virtue is moral excellence, or moral worthiness, and is, therefore, a thing preëminently of the heart. The virtuous man must not only do the right, but love the right. He must be possessed of such principles and dispositions as incline him to the right, and fortify him against temptations to the wrong. Virtue is the sum of all moral excellence, whether in character, principles, or conduct. It is, therefore, if not "the pearl of great price," the next thing to it — the most precious of all things earthly.

3. *Of virtue and the virtues.* — Virtue, as we have seen, is, externally, doing right, and, internally, intending right. It is, therefore, the principle of right deep-seated and established in the heart — that reverence for the right which brings all the thoughts, words, actions, and feelings into subjection to it, and moulds the whole character after the model of the highest perfection. The general principle of virtue, then, is, to be right and to do right

in all things. The principle is thus one. But this principle, manifested in any particular department of life, may very properly be called *a* virtue, and thus there may be a variety of virtues. The four cardinal virtues have already been enumerated and considered, and there are many others under these. These virtues, however, are not to be considered merely as so many *separate habits*, but as equally the fruit of the general principle of virtue. The principle of habit, or the fact that repetition produces an increased tendency to action in any direction, is an important aid to virtue when it has become habitual, as it is an aid to vice when that has become habitual; it is, however, in itself, neither virtuous nor vicious, but only a law of our nature, which ought, indeed, to be engaged in the service of virtue, as every other principle of our nature should. While, therefore, there are many virtues, the principle of virtue is one; and hence he who shows a deficiency in any one virtue, to the same extent shows a deficiency in the virtuous principle. It is on this ground that the apostle James says, "Whosoever shall keep the whole law, and yet offend in one point, he is guilty of all."

SUPPLEMENT.

HISTORICAL ABSTRACT OF OPINIONS ON THE GROUND OF RIGHT AND WRONG.

1. SINCE Ethics, as a theory, has to do wholly with the ground of right and wrong, an abstract of the views of the most eminent moralists on this central doctrine of the science will form a fitting supplement to the preceding treatise. Accordingly, it is here proposed to set forth, as far as may be in chronological order, some of the more prominent opinions which have been held, in different ages, and by different speculators, as to the ground of right, or the nature or principle of virtue. Opinions on other points will be referred to only incidentally, and as they bear upon the main doctrine.

2. In such an abstract we need go no farther back than Socrates, (about 450 B. C.) The Grecian sages before him had cultivated physical philosophy chiefly, confining their speculations almost wholly to the origin and nature of things. Coming on to the stage of action contemporaneously with the Sophists, who, as teachers of the art of success, seem to have subordinated morality, as they had philosophy, to effect in speaking and acting, Socrates appears to have felt the necessity of a more formal and distinct enunciation of the grounds both of knowledge and of virtue. To establish a solid ground for virtue, he appealed from individual opinion to the general convictions of men, and maintained the doctrine that the right is as certain, and as much a science, as the truth; nay, more, that they are the same; and hence, that virtue is but wisdom in action. According to his theory, the truly wise man will be a virtuous man. He thus makes virtue independent of utility, by giving it a foundation in nature, like the

truth. But at the same time, he vitiates his whole system by not allowing for the influence of passion, habit, and wrong biases. Experience shows that one may "know the right and approve it too," may "hate the wrong, and yet the wrong pursue."

3. In the doctrines of the schools of Megara and Cyrene, which sprang, by opposite tendencies, from the Socratic teachings, we find the beginnings of two opposing systems of morals, which have ever since divided the opinions of moralists, and which became especially famous under the rival sects of the Stoics and Epicureans. The Megaric philosopher Stilpo, by teaching that the highest attainable excellence consists in a profound impersonal *indifference*, first suggested the Stoical doctrine of *apathy*, which afterwards became so famous, as the symbol of a theory of morals, which made virtue wholly independent of happiness. On the other hand, Aristippus of Cyrene, in putting forth the doctrine of "Pleasure the Chief Good," made

pleasure the rule of right, and laid the foundation for the more rational system of the Epicureans, that a well-regulated happiness is the rule of right.

4. Plato, as "the beloved disciple," more truly reflects the moral, as he does also the metaphysical, principles of Socrates, than any of his successors. The spirit of his philosophy, like that of his master, is eminently ethical. It proposes as its object the purification of the soul by the contemplation of ideal truth and excellence. In his view, the True, the Beautiful, and the Good are all one; or rather, the two former are merged in the latter, — the true and the fair both alike minister to the good. The good or the perfect is alike the end of both. The study of truth, therefore, is the study of goodness; and philosophy is the purification of the soul. This is only carrying out to its consequences the doctrine of Socrates, that knowledge is virtue. True happiness, too, was the fruit of philosophy, with Plato, as it had

been of wisdom or virtue, with Socrates. Thus philosophy was the chief good with him, but only because it was the pursuit of the good through the true. Indeed, the good was the end of God himself, both in making the world and in all his acts. The good determined all his actions, as it should those of men.*

5. Aristotle, a disciple of Plato, the next great name in the history of Grecian philosophy, departed considerably from his master in ethics, as he did in other branches of philosophy. He placed morality in doing, rather than in knowing, and recognized much more distinctly than his master the influence of the passions and affections. Still, he requires that the passions and affections should be under the control of reason, in order to be right. Passion, or feeling, as the impulse to action, may be deficient, or it may be in excess; but there is a certain just exercise of

* This paragraph has been transferred from the Appendix to my Intellectual Philosophy, as have, also, a few other paragraphs in this abstract.

the passions sanctioned by reason, which is virtuous. Virtue, therefore, with him, was a mean between two extremes — it was moderation in all things.

6. Advancing now to the rival sects of Stoics and Epicureans, which fill so large a space in the history of Greek philosophy, we find the great ethical principle of the former to have been, that virtue is acting according to nature. For, as the order of nature is the will of God, to act according to it is the highest virtue. Conduct, then, should be controlled by reason taking a calm and comprehensive survey of the order of nature, and not by impulse or the love of pleasure. Happiness and all external advantages were regarded by them as mere accidental concomitants of action, not as a real good, or end of nature. The system not only placed happiness below the right, but disregarded it altogether, and endeavored to replace all emotion by a profound indifference and apathy.

7. The ethical doctrines of the Epicureans

were an exaggeration in the opposite direction. As the Stoics rejected happiness altogether, as an end of life, the Epicureans made it the chief end of life; not, indeed, the happiness of unrestrained gratification, of whatever sort, like the Cyrenaic school; but yet, mere happiness, as such. Epicureanism was not a system of mere sensualism or momentary indulgence, but rather of self-interest. It required a subordination and systematization of the different kinds of happiness, but only as such a course is necessary in order to attain the greatest amount of happiness on the whole. Conduct was to be regulated, but by no higher standard than that of an enlightened self-interest. It recognized no immutable law of right and wrong, and hence left each one to be governed by the wholly uncertain standard of his individual conception of what was for his own good. At the same time, it made happiness consist largely in the absence of pain and care; and hence exempted the gods from all interest or concern in the affairs of men.

8. Nothing of any considerable significance, in an ethical point of view, emerged in the subsequent developments of Greek philosophy, either on Grecian soil, or later, at Rome. Cicero, though an extensive reporter of Grecian philosophy and ethics, added nothing of importance of his own. Indeed, he appears to have held distinctly to no particular system, though more of an Academician than any thing else. The Schoolmen, also, of the middle ages, proposed no new system of morals, being devoted to theology rather than ethics. Indeed, we find no new contributions to the theory of morals, of any importance, till the time of Cromwell, when Thomas Hobbes published his "Leviathan." The real principle of this book is, that might is right, and conscience only fear. He regards mutual hostility, or war, as the natural state of man, and civil government as the only restraint upon this. He denies any natural distinction between right and wrong, ascribing the distinction which is observed between them

wholly to law and custom. Virtue, then, is simply obedience to the powers that be; and that, too, for the sake of the benefit to be derived thence.

9. In France, the principles of Hobbes were embraced by Gassendi, and gradually carried out to their consequences by the subsequent writers, who brought on the corruption in morals and religion which ended in the French revolution. The advantage, or happiness, which Hobbes regarded as the end of virtue, was gradually lowered down till it became simply momentary sensual pleasure. And, as might have been expected, the whole movement ended in the denial of all morality, and, indeed, of religion even, and the very existence of God.

10. In England, on the contrary, the views of Hobbes were generally rejected and opposed, and this on two different grounds; one class of writers admitting happiness, or well-being, to be the proper end of action, but regarding virtue as the essential condition of

this well-being; while the other class of writers held that right is in itself the proper rule and end of action. Henry More and Richard Cumberland are representatives of the former class of writers, while Ralph Cudworth and Samuel Clarke stand as representatives of the latter.

11. More, in his *Enchiridion Ethicum*, defines ethics to be, *the art of living well and happily;* but this happiness must spring primarily from virtue, not from sensual enjoyment. In like manner, Cumberland, in his *Disquisitio de Legibus Naturæ*, takes the ground that a universal benevolence of each to all is the true law of nature in regard to man's actions. Such a law is shown to tend to the greatest happiness of all, and hence, it is inferred, must be the law of God, as well as the law of nature. Thus, with both these writers, virtue was but a means to the further end of happiness.

12. Cudworth and Clarke, on the contrary, made virtue an end in itself. This is indicated, in the case of the former, by the very

title of the treatise in which his ethical views are set forth most fully—"A Treatise concerning Eternal and Immutable Morality." In this treatise, good and evil, justice and injustice, are held to be independent of all law, of all mere tendency to happiness, and, indeed, of every thing else, except the mind perceiving them. Dr. Clarke, although he wrote no treatise expressly upon the subject of morals, yet set forth his ethical views very distinctly in several tracts on other subjects. He makes moral distinctions depend upon the fitness and unfitness of things. As God is determined in his acts by a view of the fitness of things, so should man be. The nature of each case renders a given course of conduct, or a certain kind of action, fit; and this fitness to the circumstances of the case may always be seen by the reason. Right, therefore, is conformity in action to the nature and reason of things, and wrong is a want of such conformity.

13. Lord Shaftesbury, the next English eth-

ical writer of any note, instead of following in the track of Cudworth and Clarke, and other writers belonging to the school of independent moralists, inclined to the morality of consequences, and adopted a doctrine of virtue very similar to that held by Cumberland. He recommends virtue, not distinctly as being right in itself, but as the greatest good, the source of the greatest happiness. At the same time, he places virtue in the exercise and gratification of the affections and dispositions which tend towards the good of others, which he says are approved, by what he calls a "reflex sense," and sometimes a "*moral sense.*" Thus Shaftesbury seems to have been the first to apply the designation *moral sense* to the moral faculty — a designation which has been extensively used ever since.

14. Francis Hutcheson, who has been called "the father of the modern school of speculative philosophy in Scotland," adopted substantially the ethical principles of Shaftesbury, which he developed in a treatise denominated

"An Inquiry into the Ideas of Beauty and Virtue." In this treatise he adopts the designation *moral sense* for the moral faculty, — which had been only incidentally employed by Shaftesbury, — as best indicating the nature of the action of conscience. With him, conscience was but a feeling or *sense* of approbation or disapprobation. At the same time, he held, with Shaftesbury, that the benevolent or kind affections are the special objects of the approbation of the moral sense, and hence constitute virtue.

15. It thus appears that virtue, among English moralists, was placed upon three different grounds — the moral sense, the nature of things, and the will of God. These different theories were stoutly maintained by their respective defenders, and were generally in sharp conflict with each other. It was under such circumstances that Warburton, in his "Divine Legation," came forward with his plan for the inclusion of all these theories in a common system. He saw nothing necessarily hostile in

these different principles, but regarded them rather as natural allies, and as each supplementing the other. By thus widening the basis, morality, as he supposed, would stand the firmer, all discord cease, and men be drawn on to virtue and happiness by a threefold cord.

16. Dr. Price* held to a strictly intuitive perception of right and wrong. According to his view, right and wrong are directly perceived by conscience, and are dependent upon nothing but the faculty by which we perceive them. They are ideas of the same class as our ideas of space, time, causation, and the like, of which we can give no account except that we are so constituted that we cannot but apprehend them as we do.

17. In Paley, on the contrary, the principle of utility, as the ground of right, appears again. He defines virtue to be "doing good to mankind, in obedience to the will of God, and for the sake of everlasting happiness."

* For Bishop Butler's view, see page 72.

Thus the *matter* of virtue is made to consist exclusively in doing good to our fellows, the *rule* of virtue in the will of God, and the *end* of virtue in the attainment of everlasting happiness. The latter, of course, as the motive to action, determines its character; and hence virtue, on his theory, is only selfishness. Still, as the right can but lead to the good, the practical rules of virtue which he deduces from his theory are usually sound and wholesome. A comparison of his practical rules of virtue with his theoretical principles shows how impossible it is for common sense to be wholly silenced by theory.

18. Jeremy Bentham, who was in part contemporary with Paley, carried out the principle of utility as the ground of right more systematically than it had been by any of his predecessors, or, indeed, by any other writer whatever. His principle of right is, *the greatest good of the greatest number.* And by good he means happiness, and, in the last analysis, pleasure. This doctrine he applies

extensively to all the departments of life, building upon it a most formidable system of individual, social, and political morality.

19. I have now only to glance at a few of the theories of morals held in other countries besides England to complete the abstract intended. And, to commence with Scotland, I need refer here only to the theories of Adam Smith, Dugald Stewart, and Sir James Mackintosh. Smith, in his "Theory of the Moral Sentiments," makes all moral distinctions depend upon *sympathy*. According to his view, we regard acts as right or wrong according as we sympathize, or fail to sympathize, with the views and feelings which actuate the agent in their performance. In like manner, also, we approve or disapprove our own acts according as we judge that others approve or disapprove them. So, too, our sense of our own and of others' merit, arises from the sense of our or their merit supposed to be entertained by others.

20. Of the two other Scottish moralists just

named, Stewart holds, with Dr. Price, to an intuitive perception of right and wrong in acts, but recognizes more distinctly the senti ments of approbation and disapprobation, or of moral beauty and deformity, consequent upon moral perceptions. Mackintosh, on the contrary, holds that our passions and affections generally, and even our sense of virtue and duty, are derived from the association of ideas. As our volitions and acts are usually prompted by either agreeable or disagreeable feelings, these acts and volitions, in turn, become themselves, by association, agreeable or disagreeable to us, and hence the direct objects of our love or repugnance. Acts and volitions, then, which are agreeable to the moral sense, are right, while those which are repugnant to the moral sense are wrong.

21. In Germany, moral questions have turned almost wholly upon the freedom of the will. On the one hand, the Pantheists and Nihilists, such as Spinoza and Hegel, really deny the possibility of virtue by denying per-

sonality, and consequently all freedom, to man. But, on the other hand, Kant and his more consistent followers make the absolute freedom of the will, in the pursuit of the right, the distinguishing characteristic of man, and the condition of all virtue. With Kant, virtue is obedience to the law of duty, enjoined by the will, against the allurements of all outward and sensuous influences. Thus his fundamental ethical doctrine is, the absolute freedom or autonomy of the will. This, being wholly spontaneous and self-determined in its action, is the legislator of the mind, and hence enacts the law of duty for life. The moral law, then, is but the law of the mind; and right, obligation, duty, are all internal, and, indeed, all the same.

22. Turning now to France, we find that ethics, as might have been expected, have partaken of the character of her psychology, and, till of late, have been chiefly of the selfish and sensual sort. Thus we saw that Gassendi eagerly embraced the ethical principles of

Hobbes; and, even before his time, La Rochefoucauld, in his "Moral Reflections and Maxims," had put forth a similar system, basing all morality upon self-love. A little later, however, the devout Malebranche taught a much loftier and purer system of morals. In his own words, (quoted by Mackintosh,) "There is one parent virtue, the universal virtue, the virtue which renders us just and perfect, the virtue which will one day render us happy. It is the only virtue. It is the love of the universal order, as it eternally exists in the Divine Reason, where every created reason contemplates it. This order is composed of practical, as well as of speculative, truth. Reason perceives the moral superiority of one being over another as immediately as the equality of the radii of the same circle. The relative perfection of beings is that part of the immovable order to which men must conform their minds and their conduct. The love of order is the whole of virtue, and conformity to order constitutes the morality of actions." Views somewhat similar to these have recently been put forth by Jouffroy, while Cousin has risen to almost Platonic loftiness and ideality in his exhibition of the good in its connections with the beautiful and the true.

23. Coming, finally, to our own country, I need refer to the theories of only a few of our more eminent moralists. President Edwards regards right as a sort of moral beauty in acts, and virtue as "benevolence to being in general." Dr. Wayland makes the *relations* of things, and Dr. Haven the *nature* of things, the ground of right, though some expressions in each of these distinguished moralists seem more consistent with the doctrine of an intuitive perception of right and wrong. To mention but a single other name, Dr. Hickok holds the somewhat peculiar view, that the right of an action consists in its *worthiness of spiritual approbation*, or conformity to the spirit's own *intrinsic excellence*.

www.ingramcontent.com/pod-product-compliance
Lightning Source LLC
LaVergne TN
LVHW011214110826
845150LV00006B/1425